Psalm 91

The Dweller

Areon Potter

WESTBOW
PRESS®
A DIVISION OF THOMAS NELSON
& ZONDERVAN

This book is a work of non-fiction. Unless otherwise noted, the author
and the publisher make no explicit guarantees as to the accuracy of
the information contained in this book and in some cases, names
of people and places have been altered to protect their privacy.

WestBow Press books may be ordered through booksellers or by contacting:

WestBow Press
A Division of Thomas Nelson & Zondervan
1663 Liberty Drive
Bloomington, IN 47403
www.westbowpress.com
1 (866) 928-1240

Because of the dynamic nature of the Internet, any web addresses or
links contained in this book may have changed since publication and
may no longer be valid. The views expressed in this work are solely those
of the author and do not necessarily reflect the views of the publisher,
and the publisher hereby disclaims any responsibility for them.

Scripture taken from the NEW AMERICAN STANDARD BIBLE®,
Copyright © 1960,1962,1963,1968,1971,1972,1973,1975,1977,1995
by The Lockman Foundation. Used by permission.

Scripture taken from the King James Version of the Bible.

ISBN: 978-1-9736-2520-9 (sc)
ISBN: 978-1-9736-2521-6 (hc)
ISBN: 978-1-9736-2519-3 (e)
Library of Congress Control Number: 2018904175

Print information available on the last page.

WestBow Press rev. date: 5/16/2018

Endorsements

Understanding who God is, and who we are in relationship to Him, is foundational to spiritual, mental, and emotional health. As a counselor, I have witnessed the profound changes that occur as a result of this understanding. In *Psalm 91—The Dweller,* Areon Potter has given a gift to believers. To the new believer, an opportunity for discovery, and to the one who has walked with God, a challenging reminder of our position in the One who is our dwelling place.

—Kathy Back, MALPC
Salem, Oregon

Areon Potter is an excellent author. After reading his first book, *From Darkness to Light,* I couldn't wait to read *Psalm 91—The Dweller.* The style Areon uses to explain dwelling makes it easy to incorporate this practice into one's life. I have found a comfort and peace as I seek that shelter that only comes from the Most High God. Thank you for another wonderful lesson in how to live a life of victory through the Lord Jesus Christ!

—Mary Mellecker, Homemaker
Phoenix, Arizona

Psalm 91 has brought a sense of comfort and peace through many difficult circumstances of my life and therefore intrigued me to read *Psalm 91—The Dweller*. In doing so, I found myself wrapped in a blanket of truth as the Lord revealed His message of what it means to dwell within His shelter, His secret place of safety—the very place I had rested many times but never understood! The author of *Psalm 91—The Dweller*, Areon Potter, has once again brought God's truth alive with his passion to teach the living Word of God. In responding to God's call upon him to deliver the message of dwelling, I have not only become equipped with the knowledge of what it means to dwell but have also chosen to incorporate dwelling as a way life—and there's no place I'd rather be!

—C. J.

Psalm 91—The Dweller is a must read for today's believer. It is obvious that Areon has heard from God and points the way in helping us understand the provision of God's shelter in our daily lives and in the midst of our darkest hours. He offers wise and applicable insight to go beyond our present state of spiritual understanding into a deeper, personal, and intimate knowledge of a loving, merciful, and just God. His verse-by-verse interpretation of Psalm 91 is timeless and intuitive while also incredibly practical for walking under God's protection in our present day world. His connections between the condition of our hearts, our personal choices, and spiritual warfare leave the reader with a sense of authority and confidence in making it personally applicable. For those who need encouragement in the midst of darkness, feel afraid, feel under constant attack, or simply need realistic insight concerning the "how to" of living life in freedom, peace, and the fullness of power in the Holy Spirit, then we need look no further. We will find each in *Psalm 91—The Dweller*.

—Brenda Kaker, Founding CEO, Everylife Inc.
Lakewood, Colorado

I have had the privilege of knowing and ministering with Areon Potter for fifteen years. I have learned things I never knew and seen things I had never imagined through the ministry of Adonai Resources. When Areon speaks, I have learned to listen. He has taken a microscopic look at Psalm 91 and closely studied its intimate details. *Psalm 91—The Dweller* has created a hunger in me to find that secret place of the Most High—where demons have no access and where I can abide in the shadow of the Almighty and experience God in His fullest.

—Pastor Joe D. "Jody" Mayes
Austin, Texas

Psalm 91

91:1   He who dwells in the shelter of the Most High Will abide in the shadow of the Almighty.

91:2   I will say to the LORD, "My refuge and my fortress, My God, in whom I trust!"

91:3   For it is He who delivers you from the snare of the trapper, And from the deadly pestilence.

91:4   He will cover you with His pinions, And under His wings you may seek refuge; His faithfulness is a shield and bulwark.

91:5   You will not be afraid of the terror by night, Or of the arrow that flies by day;

91:6   Of the pestilence that stalks in darkness, Or of the destruction that lays waste at noon.

91:7   A thousand may fall at your side, And ten thousand at your right hand, But it shall not approach you.

91:8   You will only look on with your eyes, And see the recompense of the wicked.

91:9   For you have made the LORD, my refuge, Even the Most High, your dwelling place.

91:10   No evil will befall you, Nor will any plague come near your tent.

91:11   For He will give His angels charge concerning you, To guard you in all your ways.

91:12   They will bear you up in their hands, Lest you strike your foot against a stone.

91:13   You will tread upon the lion and cobra, The young lion and the serpent you will trample down.

91:14   "Because he has loved Me, therefore I will deliver him; I will set him securely on high, because he has known My name.

91:15   He will call upon Me, and I will answer him; I will be with him in trouble; I will rescue him, and honor him.

91:16   With a long life I will satisfy him, And let him see My salvation." (Psalm 91:1–16)

To those who have stood fast in the face of adversity and boldly proclaimed their trust in God regardless of prevailing circumstances.

To those who would make the choice to dwell in the shelter of the Most High and abide in the shadow of the Almighty.

May God give you wisdom, knowledge, and understanding on your journey.

Contents

About the Author

Areon Potter was raised in Dorris, California, a small town nestled a few miles from the southern Oregon border. After receiving a call from Uncle Sam and serving four years in the US Air Force, Areon received a bachelor of arts degree from Northwest Nazarene College in Nampa, Idaho. While there, he met and later married his wife, Carol. The couple moved to Nevada, where he worked with delinquent youth as a supervisor/teacher for nearly nine years. While working in Nevada, Areon sensed a call to enter into the realm of Christian counseling, and he accepted an internship with Grace Fellowship International in Denver, Colorado, in the spring of 1980. Upon completion of the internship, the organization offered Areon a counseling position. He accepted the invitation, and the family officially moved to Denver, where they settled down to raise their two sons. While in Denver, God began teaching Areon how the flesh and our spiritual enemies work in the lives of believers.

In 1985, Areon and Carol founded Adonai Resources, a counseling ministry that teaches Christians to deal with the flesh and with the oppressive assaults of the enemy. In 1992, Areon sensed God directing him to author his first book, *From Darkness to Light*, which addresses the issue of demonic oppression and the Christian.

Foreword

Areon Potter's study on Psalm 91 could not have been written at a more appropriate time in our history. Taking so much for granted has created much uncertainty in our lives. Our jobs, our finances, and our retirement plans are being stripped away; our secure world is being shaken. Where does one go for stability in this unstable world? Down through the ages, people have turned to Psalm 91 for comfort and strength. This psalm is loaded with spiritual insight and makes reference to dwelling, abiding, and the need to enter into the secret place of the Most High. What does it mean to be a dweller? Many questions will be answered in this tremendous book.

- What is the secret place?
- Where is the secret place?
- How do I enter the secret place?
- What will I find in the secret place?

When all your security is threatened, Psalm 91 is the shelter you need. *Psalm 91—The Dweller* explains how you can become a dweller as you traverse the storms of life. May the Lord unlock the wonderful truths of the psalmist's timely words as you begin your journey through *Psalm 91—The Dweller*. May you truly learn to dwell in the shelter of the Most High and abide in the shadow of the Almighty.

—Dr. Jim Logan Biblical Restoration Ministries
Sioux City, Iowa

Psalm 91—The Dweller Study Guide
is available from the author.
Great for individual or group study.
152 coil-bound pages
8.5 in. x 11 in.
$17.95
Other books written by Areon Potter include
From Darkness to Light and
From Darkness to Light Study Guide.
Great for individual or group study.
168 coil-bound pages
8.5 in. x 11 in.
$17.95

Areon Potter
areon@adonairesources.org
www.adonairesources.org

Acknowledgments

I first became aware of Psalm 91 when my wife and I were invited to attend a seminar on spiritual warfare. The speaker briefly referenced the four names of God found in the first two verses of the ninety-first psalm. As I began investigating the psalm more thoroughly on my own, I started to share what I was learning with a small church group. We learned many significant truths as we studied through Psalm 91. I am grateful for their input, patience, and kind words as we worked our way through the psalm's text. The group's encouragement prompted me to put into writing what I learned.

I thank Les and Kathy Back, Linda Knight, and my wife, Carol, for taking time to read, critique, and offer suggestions for the manuscript.

I am also deeply appreciative to those who have partnered and supported the ministry of Adonai Resources both prayerfully and financially over the years. Your prayers and financial contributions have enabled us to continue our involvement in the work God has called us to do.

With deep gratitude,
Areon Potter

Introduction

This study began when I initially realized the first two verses of Psalm 91 contained four different names for God. As I began looking deeper into the meaning of the psalm, I developed a new appreciation for the significance of what the psalmist had recorded. Although it is Old Testament, the ninety-first psalm gives a clear picture of the life of a New Testament Christian who wants to follow God to the fullest extent possible.

The psalm contains only sixteen verses but shows an important progression in the life of the person who wishes to dwell in the shelter of the Most High and abide in the shadow of the Almighty. It is not a leisurely walk down a serene path. Rather it is an expedition that requires commitment, faith, and perseverance. Although the journey does not begin automatically, all believers would benefit from such a pilgrimage. Conversely, not all believers will desire or consciously choose to begin such a journey.

Scripture informs us that during our earthly conflict, we wage war against three enemies—the world, the flesh, and the devil. Although the verses in Psalm 91 can be effectively applied to all three enemies, the psalm more clearly illustrates the dweller's encounter and assured victory over spiritual enemies. These adversaries employ both the world and the flesh in their diverse attacks upon the followers of Christ.

The entire ninety-first psalm hinges upon the announcement of the first verse. "He who dwells in the shelter of the Most High will abide in the shadow of the Almighty." The psalmist states that it is "he who dwells" that "will abide in the shadow of the Almighty." In other words, if one desires to abide in the shadow of the Almighty, he must first learn to dwell in the shelter of the Most High. If the dwelling does not take place, neither shall the abiding. According to verse 1, dwelling is prerequisite to abiding.

After making his own qualifying declaration as a dweller in the second verse, the psalmist speaks to another person in the third verse. "For it is He who delivers *you*." He then proceeds through verse 8 to present the process by which a person can enter into a lifelong experience of dwelling in the shelter of the Most High and abiding in the shadow of the Almighty.

A transition takes place in verse 9. The tenor of the psalm takes a significant turn as the psalmist's student appropriates dwelling as a way of life. In verses 10 through 13, the psalmist proceeds to delineate the awesome rewards of a life of dwelling in the shelter of the Most High while abiding in the shadow of the Almighty. In the last three verses of the psalm, the psalmist records four magnificent, God-given promises to the dweller. These verses clearly show that God is well-pleased with him and enables him to abide in the shadow of the Almighty.

Psalm 91—The Dweller is a study of the ninety-first psalm, and its purpose is to enlighten the reader to the truths that are hidden below the surface. It is apparent by the end of the psalm that God is delighted with the growth in the life of the dweller and the outcome of the journey he has traversed. As a result, the Most High, the Almighty, the righteous judge, the Creator makes some rather astounding, life-impacting promises on his behalf. In order to be able to understand spiritual issues, our heart and our understanding must be right. Spiritual understanding enables Christians to perceive truth as the Holy Spirit reveals it. May God's Spirit give you understanding as you ponder the meaning of the psalmist's words and consider the journey before us.

My prayer for you, the reader, is ...

That the God of our Lord Jesus Christ, the Father of glory, may give to you a spirit of wisdom and of revelation in the knowledge of Him. I pray that the eyes of your heart may be enlightened, so that you may know what is the hope of His calling, what are the riches of the glory of His inheritance in the saints, and what is the surpassing greatness of His power toward us who believe. (Ephesians 1:17–19a)

Notes

Psalm 91:1

Dwelling in the Shelter of the Most High
Part 1

He who dwells in the shelter of the Most High
Will abide in the shadow of the Almighty.

There are promises that are unconditional, and there are those that are conditional. Unconditional promises are given with no strings attached. For example, if a father announces to his family that they will be going to Hawaii for vacation on the fourth of June, the family has received an unconditional promise, and they can begin making plans.

We are all aware, however, that many promises have specific conditions attached. For example, a mother may promise her four-year-old son an ice cream cone after he picks up his toys. A football coach may tell one of his second-string players that if he excels in practice, he will make the team. An employer may promise an employee a generous bonus in his or her next paycheck if a certain quota is met. When the conditions are met, the conscientious person can expect to receive what was promised—whether the reward is an ice cream cone, making the team, or getting a bonus once an established quota has been met.

The first verse of Psalm 91 incorporates two elements—a condition and a promise. The condition is first stated, "He who dwells in the shelter of the Most High…" The promise follows, "[he] will abide in the shadow of the Almighty." Although the promise is available to all believers, it is not an automatic provision that is granted at the moment of salvation. It is our right, privilege, and honor as Christians to dwell in the shelter of the Most High. However, demonic forces know we cannot listen to them and dwell in the shelter of the Most High simultaneously.[1] Consequently, the forces of darkness want us to dwell on their lies, thoughts, and feelings. When people make the choice to receive Jesus Christ as their personal Savior, the kingdom of darkness suffers a major loss, and it loses one of its own to the One they hate. Although God has a plan for the people who bear His image, the usurper also has a plan that is much different and destructive. Thus, it is important for the would-be dweller to learn to take every thought captive to the obedience of Christ.

He Who Dwells

Speaking of the incarnation of Jesus, the book of John introduces a remarkable statement in the first chapter.

> And the Word became flesh, and dwelt among us, and we beheld His glory, glory as of the only begotten from the Father, full of grace and truth. (John 1:14)

The word *dwelt* in the previously outlined verse is defined as "to pitch a tent, to tabernacle."[2] Although Jesus was born a Savior, He pitched His tent and dwelt among us for thirty-three years before He saw the completion of His God-given mission on the earth.

The word rendered *dwells* in Psalm 91:1 means "to dwell, sit, abide, inhabit, remain."[3] *Dwells* is a verb and shows action. It is something we do. We dwell. We can manage our lives from our souls or from our spirits. If the world, the flesh, or the kingdom of darkness can somehow influence us to operate (or dwell) from our souls, our enemies regain much lost ground. Hence, the battle. If we operate according to the dictates of the Holy Spirit, who lives in our spirits,[4] the enemies' assaults on our lives will be effectively countered and squelched. In league with the world and the flesh, demons will do whatever they can to prevent believers from dwelling, sitting, abiding, inhabiting, or remaining in the shelter of the Most High. Thus, they are able to prevent us from abiding in the shadow of the Almighty.

He Who Dwells *in the Shelter*

To "dwell in the shelter of" implies that there is a qualified need or purpose for some type of protection and that it must be available. To some degree, that means there must be the probability of a siege of some proportion. Such an assault could negatively influence or threaten people in such a way that they should recognize the importance of having access to some type of safe haven. This psalm's first verse acknowledges that a shelter is indispensable, but it is also accessible.

A shelter is something that covers or affords protection. Going into a building, into your car, or into your home during severe weather might be an example. My wife and I have friends living in Oklahoma who have experienced severe weather. During one such storm while the husband was safely working in another part of the city, a tornado struck. Minutes before the twister hit, our friends' daughter and granddaughters had persuaded their mother/ grandmother to seek safety in their neighbor's underground shelter. Had they not all been under the storm shelter's protection, they most likely would have been severely hurt or killed. The tornado destroyed their home.

During the course of severe weather such as a tornado or hurricane, it is wise to stay in a secure shelter until the dangerous weather passes by. During the storm our friends were safe in a protective shelter. The shelter was not their own. It belonged to their neighbor. Thankfully, our friends had access to that shelter in their time of need. In like manner, dwellers do not dwell in a shelter at all times. After sensing the probability of some imminent spiritual attack, they go into the shelter of the Most High.

The shelter of the Most High spoken of in this first verse of Psalm 91 is not referring to a location where God is safe. Although He does dwell in His shelter, the Most High is not there because of any danger from His enemies. This shelter is simply a location that belongs to the Most High, and He has given believers access to that shelter. Where is this shelter of the Most High? Your Christian friends might supply you with a variety of answers. Some say the church is the shelter. Some declare the shelter to be praise. Others assert the shelter of the Most High to be in heavenly places. Regardless, the shelter of the Most High must be a place where we can be with Him.

In order for it to be a safe place for the believer, this shelter must also be a place where fallen angels cannot go. That would certainly eliminate the mind as being the shelter of the Most High.

Scripture confirms that a human being consists of three major components—a spirit, a soul, and a body that comes in various sizes, shapes, and colors.[5] Our spirit relates to God. Our soul relates to others. And our body is the tent in which we live and relate to the world around us. In Ephesians 2, we read about this relationship.

> But God, being rich in mercy, because of His great love with which He loved us, even when we were dead in our transgressions, made us alive together with Christ (by grace you have been saved), and hath raised us up together, and made us sit together in heavenly places in Christ Jesus. (Ephesians 2:4–6)

These verses tell us that although we were separated from Christ, God in His mercy gave believers new life and raised us and seated us with Him in heavenly places. Notice that these verses in Ephesians 2 were written in the past tense. Believers have already been raised and seated with Christ in heavenly places. There are no further requirements. It has been done for them. If you are a believer, you have been seated with Christ in heavenly places. That is true of all believers regardless of their circumstances, situations, or feelings. What part of us has been raised and seated in heavenly places with Christ? A Christian's spirit has been raised and seated in heavenly places in Christ Jesus.

The soul is our personality. The soul expresses itself through the functions of the mind, the emotions, and the will. Although a Christian's spirit may reside in heavenly places in Christ Jesus, one's mind and body are required to tough it out here on earth while dealing with the affairs of everyday life.

This raises an interesting question. Are we residing in the shelter of the Most High when we are frequently overwhelmed with what is going on in our lives on a daily basis? In other words, are we dwelling in the shelter of the Most High when we make decisions based solely upon our mental reasoning or emotions? A review of a biblical account in the life of Elijah, a prophet of the LORD, will help answer that question.

- **Mental Reasoning or Emotions**

Israel had forsaken the commandments of the LORD and had chosen to follow the Baals. Elijah told King Ahab, the king of Israel, that there was going to be a drought in the land, and the land of Israel went without rain or dew for about a three-year period. As the drought worsened, King Ahab became quite upset with the prophet and wanted desperately to locate him in order to solve the current water famine.

When Elijah finally made contact with Ahab, he told the king to gather all Israel on Mount Carmel for a showdown.

Once everyone was in place, Elijah spoke to the people. It was time to make a choice. They needed to decide whom they would worship—Baal or God. He instructed the prophets of Baal to place their sacrifice upon an altar and to call upon their god. Elijah would do the same. The one who answered by fire would be God. The people thought Elijah's idea was a good one.

After giving the contending prophets all the time they needed with nothing happening, Elijah prayed a short prayer, and God answered by sending fire that completely consumed his sacrifice. As a result, the people agreed that the Lord really was God.

It did not take King Ahab long to inform Queen Jezebel about the confrontation on Mount Carmel and the fact that Elijah had slain all her prophets. Jezebel was not happy when she heard the news and quickly dispatched a message to Elijah telling him he would be as dead as her prophets within twenty-four hours. We might expect Elijah to respond by calling down fire from heaven to cook Jezebel's goose. However, that was not Elijah's strategy. Instead he made a decision based upon his mental reasoning and emotions, and he ran in fear for his life into the wilderness and wanted to die.

While Elijah was operating from his spirit and intuitively receiving instruction from the Lord, he stood firm with a confident faith. Once he began leaning upon the rationale provided by his own thinking and emotions, his faith faltered, and he ran for his life.

Although God expects us to utilize our mind and emotions, Christians cannot be dwelling in the shelter of the Most High while making decisions based solely upon their mental reasoning or emotions. That is what Elijah was doing at the time. In order to dwell in the shelter of the Most High, we must receive and utilize information that resides in our spirit.

- **Circumstances**

Are we dwelling in the shelter of the Most High when we make decisions based upon our circumstances? King David provides us with a tragic example.[6] After sending his troops to battle, the king was walking about on the roof of his house and saw a beautiful woman bathing. Her name, he discovered, was Bathsheba. As he watched, his interest was stimulated. The king sent for her, even though his servants had told him she was married. During the course of events, Bathsheba conceived. Once she informed the king of her condition, he sent for her husband, who was with the army. The king then tried to tempt him to go home to be with his wife with the hope the two would engage in the act of marriage. However, Bathsheba's husband, Uriah, would not even enter his house because of the war. While his fellow soldiers were putting their lives on the line, he refused to enjoy the pleasures of marital bliss even for an evening or two. Instead he chose to stay with the servants of the king, much to the chagrin of King David. In an attempt to counter Uriah's actions, King David sent for the faithful soldier and enabled him to become inebriated. Still, Uriah refused to enjoy the pleasures of married life while on leave.

King David then wrote a letter and instructed Uriah to deliver it to Joab, the commander of the army. In the letter the king told Joab to put Uriah in the heat of the battle where he was certain to be killed. The commander followed the orders of his king, and shortly thereafter, Uriah, the husband of Bathsheba, was dead.

King David had made a series of decisions based upon his circumstances. For whatever reason, King David did not go to war with his army but remained in Jerusalem. His circumstance, however, gave him opportunity to fulfill his upcoming desire any way he wished. That decision led to other choices in an attempt to cover up the consequences of his original decision. Because of King David's actions, the LORD was displeased and declared the actions of the king to be evil. At the time, King David was not dwelling in the shelter of the Most High. Instead he made decisions based upon the urges of his body and had taken full advantage of his circumstances to fulfill the desires of his flesh.

We might ask if there were any ramifications for David's choices. Although Bathsheba did later marry the king, the son she conceived died because David had given the enemies of the LORD occasion to blaspheme. Because he was guilty of adultery and murder, the LORD told him through the prophet Nathan that the sword would never depart from his house.[7]

We, too, can look at our circumstances and make ungodly decisions based upon what transpires around us. Instead, if we do not wish to encounter the discipline of the Lord, we need to look at our situation from God's perspective and make choices that are in accord with His will.

• **Obedience**

Are we dwelling in the shelter of the Most High when we make decisions based upon what God says? The LORD had told Jonah to go to Nineveh and give them a warning concerning their wickedness. However, Jonah had other ideas. He decided to run from the LORD and gained passage on a ship headed for Tarshish. All was going well until a great storm hit and threatened to destroy the vessel. The sailors called upon their gods to calm the waters, but the storm continued to rage. When the captain approached Jonah, he found him sleeping in the belly of the ship. He woke him and asked him to call upon his god. The captain was hoping Jonah's god would be concerned about their plight. When the sailors cast lots to find the one responsible for all the trouble they faced, the lot fell upon Jonah. God's runaway told them he was the cause of the storm. Furthermore, he informed them that if they would throw him overboard, the sea would become calm.

After unsuccessfully trying to get the struggling vessel to shore, the storm intensified until the crew took Jonah's strange advice and threw him overboard. Although the sea stopped its raging, Jonah found himself in the belly of a great fish for three days and three nights. He chose to rethink his decision and began to pray—rather sincerely. As a result, God instructed the fish to vomit Jonah onto the dry land.[8]

When Jonah's feet hit the sandy shore, they were headed for Nineveh, and he immediately began proclaiming the message that the LORD had given him. Moreover, the people were listening. When the message reached the king, he issued a proclamation that required the inhabitants of Nineveh to call upon God and to turn from their wicked ways. The city of Nineveh repented. The angels rejoiced.

You would think that Jonah would be walking on cloud nine. Instead he was displeased and angry. Although it required a little time, some special circumstances, and a little persuasion, Jonah had obeyed God, but his heart was not right. Jonah was not dwelling in the shelter of the Most High. Dwelling from his emotions, he wished he could die.

Although making decisions based upon what God says is critical to dwelling, we are not yet dwelling in the shelter of the Most High just because we are being obedient. Obedience does not define dwelling, although it is a prerequisite. Obedience might qualify as a requirement for walking after the Spirit. However, as we have seen from the book of Jonah, a Christian can be obedient to God and still not be dwelling in the shelter of the Most High.

- **An Example of Dwelling**

Let us look at a situation that involves dwelling. Caleb and Joshua found themselves on an important mission.[9] Moses sent a twelve-man envoy on a forty-day journey to spy out the land of Canaan, the future Promised Land of the children of Israel. Upon their return, they were to give their report. After seeing the produce of the land, they all agreed that it was a land of plenty. Consensus was lacking, however, when it came to the prospect of conquering the inhabitants of the land. Ten of the twelve thought it to be an unwise choice; they saw the occupants as being far too strong.

The congregation heard the ten spies' report. They bemoaned their situation, thinking it would have been a far better plight had they remained under Pharaoh in Egypt. They were not only angry with Moses and Aaron, but they were also mad at God and questioned His intention for taking them out of Egypt in the first place.

Joshua and Caleb were the only dissenters of the twelve. Their positive report assured the people that the LORD was with them, and that their campaign would be successful. Unfortunately, their comments did not sway the people. Instead the people were ready to start flinging stones.

The ten spies that had given their evil report later died of a plague—as did those who were older than twenty and had grumbled against God. They died in the wilderness and never saw the Promised Land.

After the death of Moses, Joshua took over leadership of the children of Israel. Forty-five years after he had given his positive report, Caleb received his inheritance. Because Caleb trusted God as his refuge and fortress, he conquered the inhabitants of the land and settled in his Promised Land. Joshua and Caleb had both followed the LORD fully. They were dwellers.

There may be times in our personal lives when the Lord leads us in a way that friends or family may oppose. If we are confident that our direction is from the Lord, we should stand firm on our resolve to follow God fully and trust Him as our refuge and fortress. In time we, too, will enter into the land God has promised.

- **An Important Insight**

The first two verses of Psalm 91 provide us with an important insight.

> He who dwells in the shelter of the Most High Will abide in the shadow of the Almighty. I will say to the LORD, "My refuge and my fortress, My God, in whom I trust!" (Psalm 91:1–2)

Notice that there are four different names given for God in these verses—Most High, Almighty, LORD, and God. Each name provides added insight into His character. The better we know the various meanings attached to God's names, the better we actually know Him. An example on the physical level might help illustrate this. Your pastor may wear different hats. You know him one way when he preaches the Word. However, you may not be aware of what he is like as a husband or father. It could be he even enjoys hunting big game, although it may be hard for you to imagine him as a hunter shooting an elk. Yet each title brings a different aspect of his character to the forefront. He is the same man but operates differently in his various roles.

In like manner, it is impossible to get a complete picture of the nature of God if we do not have some understanding of His various names. Some say God is love, and He is. However, He is also a God of justice.[10] God uses different names in order to give us a glimpse into His character. For the purpose of this study, we will briefly highlight the names for God that have been disclosed in the first two verses of Psalm 91.

He Who Dwells in the Shelter
of the Most High

The first name for God mentioned in this first verse is the Most High. The Hebrew word for *Most High* is *El Elyon*, which reveals that God is the highest. All others are below Him. El Elyon (or the Most High) is the highest of the high. He is the possessor of heaven and earth.

The first mention of the Most High is found in the book of Genesis when Abram's nephew and his family lived in Sodom. They had been captured and taken hostage by Chedorlaomer, king of Elam, with the help of three other kings of the region. Once Abram was informed of the calamity, he mustered his trained men. Abram then pursued his nephew's captors, defeated them, and regained possession of everything the four kings had stolen and kidnapped. On his way home, Melchizedek, the king of Salem, met Abram. The king was a priest of El Elyon, the Most High. King Melchizedek blessed Abram and told him the Most High had delivered Abram's enemies into his hand.[11]

We can see a little known characteristic of God brought into clear focus from this incident in the life of Abram. The Most High is interested in delivering our enemies into our hand. He assures our victory and causes our enemies to experience certain defeat.

Lucifer, who disguises himself as an angel of light,[12] fostered a lofty although errant desire to be like the Most High. In an attempt to achieve his goal, he persuaded one-third of the angelic host to join him. Their decision was final and sealed their fate. Never again would they enjoy being in the presence of the Most High. Their hatred for Him is clearly revealed as they spin their web of deceit, lies, and rebellion in the lives of humanity. Regardless of their disdain for El Elyon, demons and their fallen leader know who He is and answer to Him, even though they stringently oppose His desires.

If what we say and do lines up with truth from God, who resides in our spirit, we have met one of the criteria to dwell in the shelter of the Most High. Nevertheless, our mind and emotions may be dwelling elsewhere. Jonah, you will recall, had delivered God's message to the people of Nineveh under duress. Although Jonah's words and actions fulfilled God's requirement and qualified him to be a dweller, his own mental reasoning and attitude did not place him in the position of dwelling in the shelter of the Most High. He was not experiencing compassion for the city of Nineveh as God had done. Rather he was dwelling in the bitterness and anger of his soul. When the circumstances of life bore down upon him, he begged to die.

• Legion

There was a foul spirit by the name of Legion that had gained control over a man.[13] The man's neighbors attempted to restrain him with chains and shackles, but it was all to no avail. He would simply break them apart and continue with his screaming and cutting himself with sharp stones. He no longer lived in his community but dwelt among the dead and in the mountains. One day the poor, tormented soul saw Jesus. He paid his respect by running to Him and bowed before Him. The foul spirit within the man then utilized the man's body and spoke to Jesus. Legion knew that Jesus was the Son of the Most High. The demonic leader had but one purpose—to refrain from going to the place of torment before the appointed time. He knew his time of torturing the man was over, and he had but one request. He wanted permission to enter into a large herd of nearby swine. As Jesus granted consent, Legion and the demons that lived in the man suddenly vacated the premises and entered into the pigs. The effect of their leaving was instant and spectacular. The once possessed man was suddenly in his right mind. He was clothed, and he wanted to remain with Jesus. The pigs, on the other hand, had departed in an unusual manner. Guided by an unseen force, they rushed down a steep bank, went into the sea, and drowned. That would no doubt qualify in *Guinness Book of Records* as the quickest way to make deviled ham.

It is clear from this account that this unclean spirit named Legion—and those under Legion's authority—could not keep from obeying Jesus, the Son of the Most High.[14] It is a comforting thought that at the name of Jesus, every knee shall bow and every tongue shall confess that Jesus Christ is Lord.[15] Demons are no exception! Toward the end of time as we know it, there will be one who rises up to dominate the entire world. He will speak out against El Elyon and will wear down His saints. His time, like Legion's, will come. Satan and his entire kingdom will be overthrown and locked in the very place Legion had so desperately wanted to avoid. Satan's aspiration to be like the Most High did not materialize!

As possessor of heaven and earth, the Most High is not concerned about the outcome of world affairs because He remains in control. Although Lucifer will never be like the Most High, believers will be conformed into His very image. In the meantime, we may experience mean times. During such stormy times, it would be wise to learn to dwell in the shelter of the Most High.

The Secret Place

The King James rendition of Psalm 91 offers a different perspective that sheds important light upon this first verse.

> He that dwelleth in the secret place of the most
> High shall abide under the shadow of the Almighty.
> (Psalm 91:1 KJV)

The King James Version uses "secret place" whereas the New American Standard Bible uses the word "shelter." In the Hebrew language, *secret place* is defined as a "covering, shelter, hiding place, secrecy."[16] When Christians are dwelling in this secret place, they are in a covering, a shelter, and a hiding place. Although the kingdom of darkness can see into the spiritual realm, demons have no access to the secret place of the Most High. The word *secret* is defined as being "kept from knowledge or view: hidden."[17] When we are dwelling in the secret place mentioned in Psalm 91:1, we are concealed in a place that is unknown to others. Psalm 27 adds clarification to the issue.

For in the day of trouble He will conceal me in His tabernacle; In the secret place of His tent He will hide me; He will lift me up on a rock. (Psalm 27:5)

The Hebrew word for *trouble* "is also used to denote evil words, evil thoughts, or evil actions."[18] It is during this day of trouble that the LORD will hide or conceal us in the secret place of His tent.

The word used here for *conceal* means to hide; to secrete; and then, to defend or protect. It would properly be applied to one who had fled from oppression, or from any impending evil, and who should be "secreted" in a house or cavern, and thus rendered safe from pursuers, or from the threatening evil.[19]

The verb *secreted* is defined as meaning "to deposit or conceal in a hiding place."[20] So where is this secret place located? First Corinthians 3 and 6 provide vital insight.

Do you not know that you are a temple of God and that the Spirit of God dwells in you? (1 Corinthians 3:16)

But the one who joins himself to the Lord is one spirit with Him. (1 Corinthians 6:17)

Or do you not know that your body is a temple of the Holy Spirit who is in you, whom you have from God, and that you are not your own? (1 Corinthians 6:19)

The New Testament reveals that the Spirit of God dwells within every believer and that those who truly worship God must worship Him in spirit and truth.[21] Since God is spirit, He joins Himself to our spirit when we are born again.[22] First Thessalonians 5 and Hebrews 4 inform us about the makeup of humanity.

Now may the God of peace Himself sanctify you entirely; and may your spirit and soul and body be preserved complete, without blame at the coming of our Lord Jesus Christ. (1 Thessalonians 5:23)

For the word of God is living and active and sharper than any two-edged sword, and piercing as far as the division of soul and spirit, of both joints and marrow, and able to judge the thoughts and intentions of the heart. (Hebrews 4:12)

Figure 1 shows the makeup of a Christian and illustrates the relationship between the spirit, the soul, and the body.

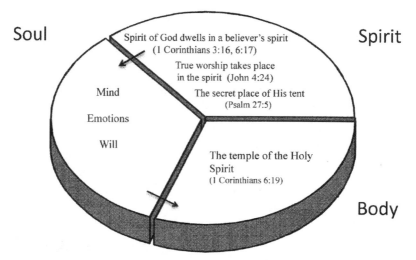

Figure 1: The Christian's Makeup

When we dwell in the shelter of the Most High, we are operating from His secret place. We are not primarily making choices or functioning according to the dictates of our mental reasoning or our emotions. Rather we are operating from our spirit, which is in cooperation with the Holy Spirit, who dwells within us. Christ is in control. Our soul is at rest, and the actions of the body are in submission to the Spirit.

Every believer has the right to dwell in the secret place of the Most High. The spirit of a believer is God's domain. When a person is born again, his or her spirit and the Spirit of God are joined together. Since we know that no evil dwells with God,[23] we can be confident that demons have no access to the spirit of a believer. Since the evil one cannot touch the Christian's spirit,[24] it behooves us to learn to dwell in the shelter—the secret place—of the Most High.

Summary

**He who dwells in the shelter of the Most High
will abide in the shadow of the Almighty.**

**He that dwelleth in the secret place of the most High
shall abide under the shadow of the Almighty.**

Psalm 91:1 (KJV)

This verse contains a condition and a promise. If believers choose to dwell in the shelter of the Most High (the condition), they will abide in the shadow of the Almighty (the promise). Although dwelling is available to all believers, not all believers are aware of that choice. A number of scenarios were given to help us understand the ramifications of dwelling and what it looked like in the life of Joshua and Caleb. We then looked briefly at the first name for God in this psalm—the Most High. We also considered what it meant to dwell in the *secret place* of the Most High as reported in the KJV.

Notes

Psalm 91—The Dweller

Psalm 91:1

Abiding in the Shadow of the Almighty
Part 2

**He who dwells in the shelter of the Most High
will abide in the shadow of the Almighty.**

**He who dwells in the shelter of the Most High
will abide ...**

We have seen that the first verse of Psalm 91 contains a condition, "He who dwells in the shelter of the Most High ..." The verse also contains a promise, "[he] will abide in the shadow of the Almighty." He who dwells ... will abide. Notice it does not say that he who dwells might abide or should abide. Nor does it say he who dwells can abide once he gets his act together. The verse is saying that if we dwell in the shelter of the Most High, we *will* abide in the shadow of the Almighty.

> The word *abide* means "to remain, lodge, spend the night, abide ... The modern Hebrew term for *hotel* is derived from this term."[25]

He who dwells in the shelter of the Most High will abide—he will rest, lodge, or remain—in that place. It is his resting place where he lodges or spends the night. He takes up his lodging there as one does in his dwelling. The New Testament helps define the word *abide* in John 8.

So Jesus was saying to those Jews who had believed Him, "If you abide in My word, then you are truly disciples of Mine; and you shall know the truth, and the truth shall make you free." (John 8:31–32)

Jesus was saying, "If you abide or continue in My word—if you tarry there, remain in it, and make My word your own—then you are truly disciples of Mine. And you will know the truth, and the truth will make you free." For the dweller, reading the Word will not be duty, drudgery, or burdensome. When we are comfortable enough to stay in the Word, learn to depend upon it, and live our lives by it, the Word will become a restful place for us. Abiding or continuing in God's Word is prerequisite to being free. Those who abide will rest, lodge, or remain in the Word. Although it may make dwellers uncomfortable at times, they will be at ease with it.

It is like going to a trusted dentist. Although it may be uncomfortable while the work is being done, we are confident that what is being accomplished will be of benefit in the end.

Scripture becomes the dwellers' resting place, and they do not mind camping in a portion of it until they gain more understanding. It is where they lodge, pass the night, and feel at home.

Remember not all promises are unconditional. Many, like John 8:31–32, have conditions attached to them. There are countless well-meaning Christians who are content to be spoon-fed but are unwilling to tarry in the Word in order to glean its hidden treasure. They are not interested in lingering in the Scriptures long enough to mine the gems contained therein. As a result, the complacent will remain in their bondage by default.

In like manner, not all believers will choose to dwell in the shelter of the Most High. They are unquestionably members of the kingdom of heaven, but they, too, will be content to forage in the shallows and remain spiritually undernourished. Unnecessarily, they will be living below their potential.

Jesus spoke of the importance of abiding.

> I am the vine, you are the branches; he who abides
> in Me, and I in him, he bears much fruit; for apart
> from Me you can do nothing. (John 15:5)

If we desire to bear much fruit as Christians, we need to abide in Christ. By so doing, we prove to be His disciples. If we do not abide in Christ, neither shall we produce anything of lasting spiritual value.

He who dwells in the shelter of the
Most High will abide *in the shadow* …

Being in something's shadow might be illustrated by walking under an umbrella on a rainy day. You would be abiding in the shadow of the umbrella, and the umbrella would be protecting you from the falling rain. Remember, a dweller does not continually live in His shelter. If that were the case, there would be no need to learn spiritual warfare. Just like a person would not stroll around under an umbrella on a warm, sunshiny day, the dweller does not live in the shelter of the Most High at all times. Nevertheless, access to that shelter is always available in time of need.

When you are shadowed by something, you are kept under surveillance. For example, if a submarine was escorting a ship, we could say the submarine shadowed the ship.

To be in something's shadow, you must be very close to it. While living in Denver, there were times when we encountered severe hailstorms. Any time the sky turned nasty, we would always ensure our car was in the garage. We could say our car was in the shadow of our garage's roof and thus under its protection. Our car was safe from the storm that would rage outside. The person who dwells in the shelter of the Most High will be very close to the Almighty and will be under His surveillance and protection.

This concept is illustrated in Genesis 19, where we find that God had sent two angels to rescue Lot and his family from the destruction of Sodom and Gomorrah. Lot saw them as they entered the city of Sodom, invited them to his home, and fed them. Before they retired for the evening, the men of the city knocked on Lot's door. They insisted that he turn over his guests so they could have sexual relations with them. After offering the group his virgin daughters, Lot said, "Do nothing to these men inasmuch as they have come under the shelter of my roof."[26] Lot was saying that the men they wanted had come under the protection of his roof and that he would not allow them to be hurt. The word *shelter* in Genesis 19:8 is defined as "shade or shadow"[27] and is the same Hebrew word that is used in the first verse of Psalm 91. He who dwells in the shelter of the Most High will abide in the *shadow* of the Almighty.

To abide in the shadow of the Almighty would be a worthy position to pursue. However, abiding in a different shadow could present an evil situation that should be avoided. Listen to the words of the prophet Isaiah.

> "Woe to the rebellious children," declares the LORD, "Who execute a plan, but not Mine, And make an alliance, but not of My Spirit, In order to add sin to sin; Who proceed down to Egypt Without consulting Me, To take refuge in the safety of Pharaoh, And to seek shelter in the shadow of Egypt! Therefore, the safety of Pharaoh will be your shame, And the shelter in the shadow of Egypt, your humiliation." (Isaiah 30:1–3)

We need to be very careful to ensure that we are not under the protection of the wrong shadow. We need to take note of a few shadows that could envelop us in an evil limelight.

• **In the Shadow of Our Ancestors**

Abiding in the shadow of your ancestors could be a challenge to overcome. If your father assassinated the president of the United

States, you would live in your father's shadow. His reputation would follow you and haunt you wherever you would go. In the spiritual realm, this is a very important element because the iniquities of the fathers are passed down to the third and fourth generations.[28] The wrong or evildoings of past generations can provide demons with the legal right to influence your life or the lives of your children and/or grandchildren.[29] For instance, if your family line has struggled with things such as immorality, lust, strife, jealousy, constant bickering and arguing, anger, or drunkenness,[30] you may find yourself waging war in the same battle zone. You may be living in the shadow of your ancestors.[31]

- **In the Shadow of an Evil Soul Tie**

Bad company corrupts good morals.[32] Therefore, an evil soul tie can overshadow a person. Have you ever been around another person who seems to affect you negatively? Perhaps they have wronged, rejected, hated, or abused you in some manner, and you become depressed, anxious, or angry when you are around them. You cannot seem to quit thinking about them in an unfavorable light. It could be you are living in the shadow of an evil soul tie.[33]

A beneficial soul tie is developed when the mind, emotions, or will of one person are bound in a healthy manner to the mind, emotions, or will of another person. In the Old Testament book of 1 Samuel, we are informed that David and Jonathan had developed healthy soul ties with each other. However, not all soul ties are healthy. When the mind, emotions, or will of one person are bound in an unhealthy manner to the soul of another person, an evil soul tie can be developed.

We find an example of a beneficial soul tie that degenerated into an evil soul tie when we look at the life of David and Israel's first king, King Saul. Samuel, a prophet of the LORD, had anointed Saul as king and had given the new leader specific instructions concerning the Amalekites that had acted with great cruelty toward the Israelites when they left Egypt. The king only partially obeyed the Lord's instruction given through His prophet. The Lord declared that Saul's partial obedience amounted to rebellion. As a result, He rejected Saul as king and instructed Samuel to anoint David as the next king of Israel. First Samuel 16 informs us of the direct consequences that came upon the rebellious king.

> Now the Spirit of the Lord departed from Saul, and an evil spirit from the Lord terrorized him. (1 Samuel 16:14)

Saul's servants advised the king that if he could find someone skilled in playing the harp, the evil spirit would depart when the instrument was played. Saul liked the concept. Therefore, when one of the young men announced David's qualifications, the king arranged for David to play his harp whenever the evil spirit oppressed the king. David's music drove the evil spirit from Saul, and the king would be refreshed. King Saul became very fond of David, and a good soul tie was soon developed between them.

About this time, the Philistines gathered for battle against Saul and his army. Their attention, however, was riveted on a giant of a man named Goliath. David's popularity grew when he volunteered to face the giant and delivered Goliath's head to King Saul. The bond between them was immediately strengthened. Shortly thereafter, King Saul set David over the men of war, and David gained favor with the king, his servants, and the people.

All was going well until Saul returned from the battle with the Philistines. As the women sang in the victory parade, they gave more honors to David than they gave to King Saul. Saul's attitude toward David quickly changed, and he began looking at him with suspicion and dread. A one-sided evil soul tie developed between Saul and David that destroyed their relationship. The angry king began an intense campaign to end David's life. As a result, David spent a portion of his life living in the shadow of an evil soul tie.

The story of King Saul and David is as relevant as tomorrow's newspaper. Their story could be applied to the lives of many Christians who experience great relationships disintegrating into a nightmarish shamble of heartbreak. Although David had no control over King Saul's life, he did not allow the king's attitude to drag him down. Instead David learned to put his trust in God. As we choose to dwell in the shelter of the Most High and abide in the shadow of the Almighty, we will overcome the devastation that can come from an evil soul tie.

- **In the Shadow of Another Person**

Beginning in Genesis 37, a story unfolds that illustrates how members of a family can come under the shadow of another family member.

Israel and his twelve sons lived in the land of Canaan. In his old age, Israel became the father of Joseph, whom he loved more than his other sons and for whom he made a colorful coat. Joseph's brothers were jealous and hated him. As a teenager, Joseph had a dream and conveyed the dream to his brothers. In the dream Joseph's sheaf stood erect, and his brother's sheaves bowed down to Joseph's sheaf. They thought Joseph's dream was absurd. However, he had another dream that they liked even less. It even caused his father, Israel, to rebuke him. In the second dream, the sun, moon, and eleven stars were bowing down to Joseph.

Sometime later, Joseph's brothers were watching their father's flock in Shechem. Their father decided to send Joseph to check on his sons and the flock. When the brothers saw Joseph coming, they concocted a plan to kill him, but Joseph's oldest brother, Rueben, modified the plan. Instead they sold him to some merchants who took him to Egypt. There he worked for Potiphar, the captain of Pharaoh's bodyguard.

After going through a variety of difficult circumstances, Joseph interpreted a troubling dream for Pharaoh that Pharaoh's staff could not decipher. Joseph interpreted the dream and informed Pharaoh of its meaning. There would be seven years of bountiful crops followed by a seven-year famine. As a reward for interpreting Pharaoh's dream, Joseph was elevated to a ruler of Egypt, second to Pharaoh himself. Pharaoh then charged Joseph with preparing for the upcoming famine. It was during the famine in Canaan that Israel sent his sons to bring grain home from Egypt. Although Joseph had been under his brothers' shadow as a teenager, the tables had turned. Israel's sons found themselves under Joseph's shadow. Joseph's boyhood dreams proved to be accurate.

Concerning a more current theme, there are women who enter into a marriage covenant only to discover the man of their dreams has somehow changed for the worse. As a result, their marriage has become a living nightmare. The man she once thought of as her prince charming turns into an abusive, unknown adversary who holds her fast in his cruel grip. He may cause her untold damage mentally, emotionally, or physically. Such women find themselves living under the shadow of an abusive, controlling brute of a husband.

- **In the Shadow of the World**

The apostle Paul talks about the *world* in the second verse of the second chapter of the book of Ephesians.

> And you were dead in your trespasses and sins, in
> which you formerly walked according to the course
> of this world. (Ephesians 2:1–2)

The planet upon which we live is not our enemy. Before God ever created man, He formed planet Earth as the place where humanity would live. Living in the shadow of the world does not refer to living on planet Earth. In *The Adversary*, Mark Bubeck provides a workable definition of "the world" as used in this context.

> As our enemy, the world is the whole organized system, made up of varying and changing social, economic, materialistic, and religious philosophies which have their expression through the organizations and personalities of human beings.[34]

Listening to the evening news frequently verifies that the world can be a very scary place. Information concerning robberies, thefts, rapes, murder, and natural disasters are commonly reported in news' broadcasts. Although our world is full of troubles, we should not be surprised. Jesus Himself told his disciples that in this world they would have tribulation.[35]

According to Thayer, "metaphorically the word *tribulation* refers to oppression, affliction, tribulation, distress, straits."[36] The word *tribulation* is translated seventeen times as "affliction."

According to Vine, *affliction* means

> "to suffer affliction, to be troubled," [and] has reference to sufferings due to the pressure of circumstances, or the antagonism of persons ... Both the verb and the noun when used of the present experience of believers, refers almost invariably to that which comes upon them from without.[37]

In the Gospel of John, Jesus spoke to His disciples.

> "If you were of the world, the world would love its own; but because you are not of the world, but I chose you out of the world, therefore the world hates you." (John 15:19)

Although we are not of the world, we must live in it for a time. Under the inspiration of the Holy Spirit, Paul gives this warning to believers in Colossians.

> See to it that no one takes you captive through philosophy and empty deception, according to the tradition of men, according to the elementary principles of the world, rather than according to Christ. (Colossians 2:8)

The King James Version of the Bible says it this way:

> Beware lest any man spoil you through philosophy and vain deceit, after the tradition of men, after the rudiments of the world, and not after Christ. (Colossians 2:8 KJV)

Albert Barnes adds a note of clarification.

> Beware lest any man spoil you—The word "spoil" now commonly means to corrupt, to cause to decay and perish, as fruit is spoiled by keeping too long, or paper by wetting, or hay by a long rain, or crops by mildew. But the Greek word used here means to spoil in the sense of plunder, rob, as when plunder is taken in war. The meaning is, "Take heed lest anyone plunder or rob you of your faith and hope by philosophy." These false teachers would strip them of their faith and hope, as an invading army would rob a country of all that was valuable.[38]

Because we are not of the world, we must be careful not to allow the philosophy of the world to take us captive or to overshadow the truth of the Word of God. The world has its own ideas, which can be quite different and opposed to those expressed in Scripture. We are not to be conformed to the world in which we live. Rather we are to be transformed by the renewing of our mind.[39] Although it may be hard to imagine, living in this world is only a temporary arrangement for the Christian. The grave is not our final resting place. When the trumpet of the Lord sounds, we will begin the rest of the story!

- **In the Shadow of the Kingdom of Darkness**

As we considered the second verse of the second chapter of the book of Ephesians, we found reference to "the world." As we examine the rest of the second verse, we find "the prince of the power of the air" or Satan and his kingdom of darkness.

> And you were dead in your trespasses and sins, in which you formerly walked according to the course of this world, according to the prince of the power of the air, of the spirit that is now working in the sons of disobedience. (Ephesians 2:1–2)

Satan declared that he would be like the Most High. Because of his rebellion against God, he was cast out of heaven and became the god of this world.[40] When a person is born into this world, by nature he becomes a part of a kingdom that is opposed to the will of God. He has no choice in the matter at this point. He is born into Satan's kingdom. In that condition he is doomed not only to a life apart from God but an eternity separated from Him. However, God had predetermined that each individual would have the right, the power, and the responsibility to choose whether they would remain in that kingdom. The antidote would be an everlasting remedy that would counteract the effects of the poisonous lies propagated by Satan and his kingdom. Jesus Christ came to this earth in the form of an infant, grew up, and shed His blood for the remission (forgiveness) of the sins of humanity. The good news is given in the Gospel of John.

> But as many as received Him, to them He gave the right to become children of God, even to those who believe in His name, who were born not of blood, nor of the will of the flesh, nor of the will of man, but of God. And the Word became flesh, and dwelt among us, and we saw His glory, glory as of the only begotten from the Father, full of grace and truth. (John 1:12–14)

Although we are born into the kingdom of darkness, we have been given the opportunity and the responsibility to choose whether we remain in that kingdom. That choice remains open until the door of death closes behind us. At that point, our decision cannot be reversed. We have either made the choice to enter the kingdom of heaven, or we will forever be banned from living in the presence of God. In the event we have never made the conscious decision to receive the Son of God's offer to pay the sin debt on our behalf, we must pay the debt ourselves. If we choose to reject Christ's offer, we will inherit the fruit of our choice and will hear these final bone-chilling words from the One who created us:

> Depart from Me, accursed ones, into the eternal
> fire which has been prepared for the devil and his
> angels. (Matthew 25:41)

However, if we wisely choose to receive God's salvation through Christ, we are immediately ushered into a new kingdom. Colossians provides the exciting details.

> For He delivered us from the domain of darkness,
> and transferred us to the kingdom of His beloved
> Son, in whom we have redemption, the forgiveness
> of sins. (Colossians 1:13–14)

Once we have been drawn by God and have surrendered our life into His hands, He transfers us out of the kingdom of darkness into the kingdom of His beloved Son. As such, we come under the direction and control of the Son of God. A major transformation has taken place, and we are no longer known as children of the devil.[41]

Scripture informs us that Lucifer declared that he would be like the Most High. Although he failed in that venture, he did become the god of this world. Yet he still desires to usurp that which does not belong to him. The word *usurp* is defined as meaning "to seize and hold in possession by force or without right."[42] Satan and his demonic kingdom desire to usurp the knowledge that believers indeed have spiritual authority over them and that they are required to utilize that authority.

Instead of exercising authority over the demonic realm, we, like Adam, can allow the kingdom of darkness to deceive us and thereby obtain an advantage as they purpose to exercise authority over us. To understand how such an unsavory thing could occur, we need only look again at John 8.

> Jesus therefore was saying to those Jews who had believed Him, "If you abide in My word, then you are truly disciples of Mine; and you shall know the truth, and the truth shall make you free." (John 8:31–32)

If the knowing of the truth makes us free, when we believe a lie, we enter into the realm of spiritual bondage. In other words, if we unknowingly believe what a demon might suggest to our mind instead of believing the truth of God's Word, demons will gain an advantage and may be able to usurp our authority. It is God's requirement that we live holy lives. If the enemy of our souls can keep us under his shadow, he can hinder us from being all that God designed us to be.

• **In the Shadow of the Flesh**

In Ephesians 2, we have already encountered the world and the devil. In the third verse, we encounter the flesh.

> And you were dead in your trespasses and sins, in which you formerly walked according to the course of this world, according to the prince of the power of the air, of the spirit that is now working in the sons of disobedience. Among them we too all formerly lived in the lusts of our flesh, indulging the desires of the flesh and of the mind, and were by nature children of wrath, even as the rest. (Ephesians 2:1–3)

Thayer defines the *flesh* in the following way:

> The soft substance of the living body, which covers the bones and is permeated with blood and applies to both men and beasts … The flesh denotes mere human nature, the earthly nature of man apart from divine influence, and therefore prone to sin and opposed to God.[43]

Paul speaks of indulging the desires of the flesh and of the mind. Colossians adds another dimension to our understanding of the word *flesh* by utilizing the word "fleshly."

> Let no one keep defrauding you of your prize by delighting in self-abasement and the worship of the angels, taking his stand on visions he has seen, inflated without cause by his fleshly mind. (Colossians 2:18)

A fleshly mind focuses on that which would appease the flesh and does not focus on that which would please the Spirit of God. As we investigate this section, we will consider *fleshly* as it is portrayed in the New Testament by the Greek word *sarkikos*, which means *fleshly* or *carnal*. Vine provides meaningful definitions.

> Speaking broadly, the carnal denotes the sinful element in man's nature, by reason of descent from Adam; the spiritual is that which comes by the regenerating operation of the Holy Spirit … Sarkikos signifies … having the nature of flesh," i.e., sensual, controlled by animal appetites, governed by human nature, instead of by the Spirit of God.[44]

Although Christians have been taken out of Satan's kingdom and have been transplanted into the kingdom of heaven, we can still find ourselves living in the shadow of the flesh. In other words, we can be living in a manner that is inconsistent with our new nature. We can, for instance, become involved with inconsistencies such as that categorized in Galatians 5 as the deeds of the flesh.

> Now the deeds of the flesh are evident, which are: immorality, impurity, sensuality, idolatry, sorcery, enmities, strife, jealousy, outbursts of anger, disputes, dissensions, factions, envying, drunkenness, carousing, and things like these. (Galatians 5:19–21)

Such actions on our part are inconsistent with our new spiritual nature as believers. When we engage in such actions, we are actually in opposition to the work that the Holy Spirit wants to accomplish in our lives. Although we may be trying to live as though we are a part of the kingdom of God, at times we may find ourselves abiding in the shadow of the kingdom of darkness and acting like the devil. Colossians tells us we need to lay these inconsistencies aside.

> But now you also, put them all aside: anger, wrath, malice, slander, and abusive speech from your mouth. Do not lie to one another. (Colossians 3:8–9)

In other words, we are not to allow our flesh to control us. We are not to be controlled by the sensual, by our animal appetites, or by our human nature. Instead we are to be governed and controlled by the Spirit of God. In 1 Corinthians 3, Paul gets to the heart of the issue.

> And I, brethren, could not speak to you as to spiritual men, but as to men of flesh, as to babes in Christ. I gave you milk to drink, not solid food; for you were not yet able to receive it. Indeed, even now you are not yet able, for you are still fleshly. For since there is jealousy and strife among you, are you not fleshly, and are you not walking like mere men? (1 Corinthians 3:1–3)

Paul just described those who have been born again but are still fleshly. They were acting no differently than the way a non-Christian might act. He referred to them as "men of flesh" and as "babes in Christ." A Christian cannot dwell in the shelter of the Most High while allowing the activity of the flesh to overshadow his new nature.

He who dwells in the shelter of the Most High
will abide in the shadow *of the Almighty.*

A believer can also live in the shadow of the Almighty. Who is the Almighty? The Hebrew rendition of the word is *El Shaddai,* and in most Bibles, the word is translated as "God Almighty" or "Almighty God."

El Shaddai is all-powerful and is able to perform that which He speaks. "*El Shaddai* is used in connection with judging, chastening and purging."[45] The ways of El Shaddai give us a clear picture of a God who is faithful to keep His covenants with His people.

We need to refresh our memories by reviewing a little history. Abram knew the LORD (Jehovah) but had not yet been introduced to El Shaddai (God Almighty). It was the LORD that had instructed Abram at the age of seventy-five to depart his country, leave his relatives, and go to a place that would later be revealed. Following the LORD's instruction Abram left his country and took his wife and his nephew with him. The LORD then made a promise to Abram in Genesis 12.

> Now the LORD said to Abram, "Go forth from your country, and from your relatives and from your father's house, to the land which I will show you; And I will make you a great nation, And I will bless you, And make your name great; And so you shall be a blessing; And I will bless those who bless you, And the one who curses you I will curse. And in you all the families of the earth will be blessed." (Genesis 12:1–3)

Moreover, Abram was blessed. Not only was there gold and silver aplenty, but also Abram and Lot's livestock had increased to the point that they had to be separated. After the two herdsmen had gone their separate ways, the LORD showed Abram the land that he had been promised. Sometime afterward, Lot was captured by some of his hostile neighbors. Fortunately, Abram came to Lot's rescue and retrieved his nephew and all his possessions.

Again, the LORD came to Abram and spoke to him in Genesis 15.

> "Do not fear, Abram, I am a shield to you; Your reward shall be very great." (Genesis 15:1)

Abram reminded the LORD that he had no offspring and was concerned that a man by the name of Eliezer would be his heir. The LORD assured Abram that he would have an heir from his own body. Then He took Abram outside and showed him the stars and told him he would have so many descendants that they would be impossible to count. Abram believed what the LORD told him. The LORD then made a covenant with Abram, assuring him that his descendants would possess the land he had been shown.

Time has a way of slipping by—and it did. With the passage of time with no child materializing, doubt did. Nevertheless, Abram's wife, Sarai, had a plan and brought her Egyptian handmaid, Hagar, into the picture. Abram went along with Sarai's plan, and Hagar soon became pregnant and found herself carrying Abram's offspring in her womb. When Abram was eighty-six years of age, Ishmael was born. Ishmael, however, was not the son that the LORD had promised.

For the next thirteen years, Sarai remained childless. By this time, Abram's and Sarai's bodies had grown old and were past the time of childbearing. When it was no longer possible for the geriatrics to bear children, the LORD came for another visit. The event is recorded in Genesis 17.

> Now when Abram was ninety-nine years old, the LORD appeared to Abram and said to him, "I am

God Almighty; Walk before Me, and be blameless. And I will establish My covenant between Me and you, And I will multiply you exceedingly." (Genesis 17:1–2)

El Shaddai then changed Abram's and Sarai's names to Abraham and Sarah. He then declared that He would bless Sarah and that she would indeed bear Abraham a son. Genesis 17 reveals Abraham's thoughts on the matter.

> Then Abraham fell on his face and laughed, and said in his heart, "Will a child be born to a man one hundred years old? And will Sarah, who is ninety years old, bear a child?" (Genesis 17:17)

By the time El Shaddai introduced Himself to Abraham at age ninety-nine, he had already lived more than half his life. Abraham would live to be 175 years of age before death would take its toll. Why the delay? Why did El Shaddai wait until he and Sarah were both over the hill to make good the promise of the LORD? Would it not seem reasonable for the child to be born while the parents were in the prime of life? Nathan Stone provides this significant insight:

> Abraham and Sarah had to learn that what God promises only God can give, that the promise was not to be made sure by the works of the flesh. So the bodies of both of them must die first to make them realize it was all of God ... Thus this name also taught Abraham his own insufficiency, the futility of relying upon his own efforts and the folly of impatiently running ahead of God.[46]

If we are to abide in the shadow of El Shaddai, we, too, need to learn that He does not need our help to bring about that which He promises. He is all-powerful and is quite capable of doing all He says He will do. The would-be dweller must first learn to dwell in the shelter of the Most High. Only then can he or she be spiritually prepared to abide in the shadow of the Almighty.

El Shaddai spoke to Abram and told him that He expected him to walk blamelessly and uprightly with integrity and sincerity and to be unblemished before Him. Those are the conditions or requirements if a person is to have a covenant relationship with El Shaddai. When that condition is met, El Shaddai promises to establish His covenant and to exceedingly multiply that person. Concerning El Shaddai, Nathan Stone says,

> *Shaddai* itself occurs forty-eight times in the Old Testament and is translated "almighty." The other word so like it, and from which we believe it to be derived, occurs twenty-four times and is translated "breast." As connected with the word *breast*, the title *Shaddai* signifies one who nourishes, supplies, satisfies. Connected with the word for God, *El*, it then becomes the "One mighty to nourish, satisfy, supply."[47]

A nursing child is naturally drawn to the mother. When hunger strikes, the mother captures the child's interest. The child goes to her, expects nourishment, and knows where to get it. The mother's milk provides sustenance and satisfies the child's appetite.

In order to abide in the shadow of the Almighty, we need to learn that El Shaddai is the One who nourishes, supplies, and satisfies. If we attempt to depend upon our own resources and be our own supply, we are not yet ready to abide in the shadow of the Almighty. Would-be dwellers must first learn to dwell in the shelter of the Most High. Only then can they be prepared to abide in the shadow of the Almighty.

According to the first verse of Psalm 91, when we dwell in the shelter of the Most High, we will abide in the shadow of the Almighty. However, the converse is also true. If we do not dwell in the shelter of the Most High, we shall not abide in the shadow of the Almighty, and we will be more vulnerable to our enemies' attacks.

- **A Satanic Counterattack**

Obviously, our spiritual enemies do not want us to dwell in the shelter of the Most High. Nor do they want us to abide in the shadow of the Almighty. Although demons know the reality and truth contained in Psalm 91:1, they try to produce just the opposite in the life of a Christian. Demons would try to counterattack believers in such a way that they would dwell under the shelter of demonic lies and abide in the shadow of the kingdom of darkness. In other words, if demons could get a person to believe their lies and to live their life in accordance with those lies, that person would then be living life in the shadow of the kingdom of darkness. Demons want to shelter us from the truth because they know God's truth will set us free from their bondage.

How much wiser it would be if those who name Christ as Savior and Lord would learn to dwell in the shelter of the Most High and abide in the shadow of the Almighty.

Summary

He who dwells in the shelter of the Most High will abide in the shadow of the Almighty.

When Christians learn to dwell in the shelter of the Most High, they enter into the promise. We found that it is possible for Christians to live in the shadow of their ancestors. They can also develop an evil soul tie and live in the shadow of another person. Furthermore, they can live in the shadow of the world, the kingdom of darkness, or the flesh. However, this first verse also promises that they can abide in the shadow of the Almighty, who is known in the Hebrew as El Shaddai. The enemy will try to prevent us from dwelling in the shelter of the Most High and has an alternate plan for us to follow.

Psalm 91:2

The Declaration

I will say to the LORD, "My refuge and my fortress, My God, in whom I trust!"

This is the starting point for prospective dwellers. Christians cannot dwell before internalizing the declaration of this verse as their own. This verse identifies the dweller's commitment or vow, which God will not take lightly.

Christians who have internalized verse 2 have learned to trust God, and their lives bear it out. They speak from experience, and what they say is not simply armchair theology. They have seen combat from the trenches and have overcome the enemy. We could paraphrase what a dweller might say to the LORD. "Concerning the LORD, here is what I have to say: 'He is my refuge and my fortress. He is my God, the One in whom I trust!'"

Verse 2 is more than just a personal commitment. It is a vow to the LORD. What does it mean to make a vow? A *vow* is defined as "a solemn promise or assertion, specifically one by which a person is bound by an act, service, or condition."[48] Dwellers have made a promise to Jehovah. "You are my refuge and my fortress." In essence, the person is saying, "I will not take refuge in my money, my job, my health, or my retirement fund. I trust You, not my health insurance, my intellect, or my circumstances." This is, indeed, very serious, and God will expect the person who makes such a vow to carry it out in a responsible manner. The book of Deuteronomy makes it very clear.

> When you make a vow to the LORD your God, you shall not delay to pay it, for it would be sin in you, and the LORD your God will surely require it of you.[49] (Deuteronomy 23:21)

Christians who have internalized verse 2 have made a vow to make the LORD their refuge and fortress. The statements found in verse 2, unfortunately, are not true of many Christians. Their refuge, fortress, and trust are in something else. What can Christians trust in other than God? They commonly trust in their paycheck, their job, their spouse, their intelligence, their talents, their resources, or whatever else they can find.

Simply because Christians verbalize verse 2 to the LORD does not make that verse experientially true. Who then is able to truthfully speak Psalm 91:2 to the LORD? Those who dwell in the shelter of the Most High can confidently declare that the LORD is their refuge and fortress. Those who dwell in the shelter of the Most High can trust in God because of what has been experientially learned and put into practice.

• Who Is the LORD?

When God spoke to Moses about sending him to Pharaoh to bring the sons of Israel out of Egypt, Moses complained that the people would not know who had sent him on his mission. Moses thought they might ask him if he knew God's name, but he was not sure what to tell them. Exodus 3 provides us with God's response to Moses's concern.

And God said to Moses, "I AM WHO I AM"; and He said, "Thus you shall say to the sons of Israel, 'I AM has sent me to you.'" (Exodus 3:14)

Ryrie comments on this name for God,

YHWH (probably pronounced "Yahweh"), [is] the most significant name for God in the Old Testament. It has a two-fold meaning: the active, self-existent One ... and Israel's Redeemer.[50]

"*Jehovah,* the English rendering of the Hebrew tetragram YHWH, [is] one of the names of God."[51] It is written as "LORD" in most translations. The book of Proverbs provides an example.

The name of the LORD is a strong tower; The righteous runs into it and is safe. (Proverbs 18:10)

You may have noticed that the word *LORD* is written in all capital letters. It is not to be confused with the Hebrew name for Adonai, which is written as *Lord* and has only the first letter of the word capitalized. For example, look at Joshua 7.

Then Joshua tore his clothes and fell to the earth on his face before the ark of the LORD until the evening, both he and the elders of Israel; and they put dust on their heads. And Joshua said, "Alas, O Lord GOD, why didst Thou ever bring this people over the Jordan, only to deliver us into the hand of the Amorites, to destroy us? If only we had been willing to dwell beyond the Jordan! (Joshua 7:6–7)

In verse 6, the word *LORD* refers to Jehovah. In verse 7, the word *Lord* in the Hebrew language refers to Adonai and reveals that Joshua is simply referring to Jehovah as his master. Nathan Stone explains,

The name *Adonai*, while translated "Lord," signifies ownership or mastership and indicates "the truth that God is the owner of each member of the human family, and that He consequently claims the unrestricted obedience of all."[52]

Psalm 9 reveals other characteristics of the LORD (Jehovah).

> The LORD also will be a stronghold for the oppressed,
> A stronghold in times of trouble; And those who
> know Your name will put their trust in You, For
> You, O LORD, have not forsaken those who seek
> You. (Psalm 9:9–10)

Not only is the LORD a stronghold for the oppressed, but He also does not forsake those who seek Him.

When Jehovah planted a garden with beautiful flowering and fruit-bearing trees, He put Adam in charge and gave Adam only one command. He was not allowed to eat from the Tree of the Knowledge of Good and Evil. He could do anything else he wanted. The LORD also gave Adam the job of naming all the animals. By doing so, Adam learned that he, too, needed a mate. The LORD caused a deep sleep to come upon Adam. He then took one of Adam's ribs and formed a helper for the garden's first inhabitant.[53] After Adam and Eve had eaten from the forbidden tree, the LORD sent them out of the garden. Furthermore, He made provision to prevent their return.

Although the LORD is a stronghold for the oppressed, Adam and Eve learned the hard way that Jehovah also condemns unrighteousness, pronounces judgment, and metes out punishment on the offenders.

I will say to the LORD, *"My refuge and my fortress …"*

> I choose him as such, and confide in him. Others
> make idols their refuge, but I will say of Jehovah, the
> true and living God, He is my refuge.[54]

A refuge is a shelter or a place of protection from danger. It is like an animal refuge where hunting is not allowed. Jehovah is a place of safety. He is a refuge. Dwellers have made a vow by declaring that the LORD is their refuge. What would God expect from those who made such a declaration? He would expect them to remain true to their word and not turn to someone or something else in search of refuge. In the language of the Old Testament, to make such a commitment and then not carry it out would amount to prostituting ourselves in the sight of God.[55]

A fortress is a fortified place. It is a place where you can safely wage a countermeasure against an enemy.[56] When we see the LORD as our fortress, we can successfully wage war against our spiritual enemies. When you are inside a fortress, an enemy must overrun or destroy the fortress to get to you. The LORD is the dweller's fortress, and no enemy can destroy Him. Therefore, the enemy will try to keep you from entering your fortress, will try to get you to leave your fortress, or will implement a plan to try to draw you out of your fortress.

**I will say to the LORD,
"My refuge and my fortress, *My God* ..."**

Who is God? *Elohim* is a plural Hebrew word usually written as "God." "Its basic meaning is strong one, mighty leader, supreme Deity."[57] What do we know about Elohim? The first chapter of the first book of the Bible introduces us to Elohim, who created the heavens and the earth and everything else that was brought into being.[58] He even created man in His own image.[59]

> Elohim refers to and implies One who stands in a covenant-relationship.[60]

In the first book of the Bible, we find a character report on a man by the name of Noah that provides an example of God entering into such a relationship.

> These are the records of the generations of Noah.
> Noah was a righteous man, blameless in his time;
> Noah walked with God. (Genesis 6:9)

In this account, we discover that God had found planet Earth to be corrupt and filled with violence. As a result, He determined to destroy those who had corrupted their ways. Since Noah walked with God, He instructed him to build an ark and gave specific instructions on how it was to be constructed. Furthermore, He informed Noah that a flood was coming that would destroy everything that had the breath of life within. God also declared that He would establish His covenant with Noah.

After the completion of the ark, God instructed Noah to take two of every kind of living thing, male and female, both clean and unclean, into the ark with him. At the appointed time, Noah, his family, and the animals entered the ark, and the LORD closed the door behind them. After waiting seven days, the flood came upon the earth, and it rained. For forty days and forty nights, it rained. Every living thing that took in breath from the air was covered in the waters of the flood. Genesis 7 provides the devastating statistics.

> Thus He blotted out every living thing that was upon the face of the land, from man to animals to creeping things and to birds of the sky, and they were blotted out from the earth; and only Noah was left, together with those that were with him in the ark. And the water prevailed upon the earth one hundred and fifty days. (Genesis 7:23–24)

Noah, his family, and all those animals were in the ark for a total of three hundred and seventy-one days (or fifty-three weeks)![61] After the waters of the flood had abated, God sent Noah, his family, and the animals out of the ark. The first action taken by Noah once his feet were on solid ground was to offer burnt offerings to the LORD.

God blessed Noah and his sons and told them to be fruitful, multiply, and fill the earth. Then God established a covenant with Noah and promised that He would never again allow a flood to destroy the earth. He also provided a sign to represent the covenant—a rainbow in the clouds. The covenant would remain in effect throughout all generations and would remind God of the promise He had made with Noah and all flesh that lived upon the earth.

This is but one example that illustrates how our God is a covenant-making God!

I will say to the LORD, "My refuge and my fortress, My God, *in whom I trust*!"

To *trust* means to have confidence in. *Trust* is defined as an "assured reliance on the character, ability, strength, or truth of someone or something. One in which confidence is placed."[62] A choice is involved when we trust. We do choose to trust, but we must also learn to trust. It is not something we do automatically. Trusting God is not as easy as it might seem. Even though our coins carry the motto "In God We Trust," the American way of life does not naturally promote trust in God.

Babies quickly learn to trust their parents as their resource for food, clothing, and other necessities of life. It is common for young children to become frightened when the parents leave them with a babysitter for the first time. As the children mature and start school, we find that their trust base increases, and this base may include significant others such as teachers, other parents, students, and friends. Although many people are reliable, children also learn that some are not.

In their teen years, these sprouting forms of humanity sometimes forget every good value they have ever learned. They may even incorporate destructive values as they desperately search for independence and significance in life.

However, look at the young man who has not fallen into the realm of bad vices. He may be a thoughtful, insightful, helpful, and industrious Christian who is also a good student. What kinds of things might this young adult have learned to trust? Not only has he probably learned to trust people, but he has also learned to trust in his capacity to think rationally and logically. He has learned to trust in his skills on the job and in the marketplace. He has learned to trust in his paycheck, his spouse, and significant others. He has the world by the tail. He would probably even make the bold declaration that he trusts God.

- **A Lesson from David's Experience**

Psalm 143 provides valuable insight from the life of David as we observe the psalmist dealing with his enemies and learning to trust God.

> Hear my prayer, O LORD, Give ear to my supplications! Answer me in Your faithfulness, in Your righteousness! And do not enter into judgment with Your servant, For in Your sight no man living is righteous. For the enemy has persecuted my soul; He has crushed my life to the ground; He has made me dwell in dark places, like those who have long been dead. Therefore my spirit is overwhelmed within me; My heart is appalled within me. (Psalm 143:1–4)

Psalm 143 should be the prayer of many Christians today who find themselves in disturbing circumstances. In the third verse of this psalm, we find that his enemies have persecuted David's soul. The word *persecution* means "to run after usually with hostile intent."[63] Because of this persecution, David's life was crushed to the ground. Referring to David's enemies, John Gill says,

> For the enemy has persecuted my soul; which is to be connected with Psalm 143:1; and is a reason why he desires his prayer might be answered, seeing his enemy, either Saul, or Absalom his own son, persecuted him, or pursued him in order to take away his soul, or life; or Satan, the enemy and avenger, who goes about like a roaring lion, seeking whom he may devour; or persecuting men, who are

his emissaries and instruments, whom he instigates to persecute the Lord's people, and employs them therein; he hath smitten my life down to the ground: brought him into a low, mean, and abject state, and near to death; had with a blow struck him to the ground, and left him wallowing in the mire and dirt, just ready to expire. The phrase is expressive of a very distressing state and condition.[64]

It was as if the enemy had beaten David down and made shambles of his life. The enemy had forced him to dwell in dark places.

His condition was like that of those who had been long in their graves; who had long since ceased to see any light; whose abode was utter and absolute gloom.[65]

The enemy had persecuted David's soul so that his thinking, his emotions, and his ability to make rational choices were in trouble. How could an enemy persecute a person's soul?

As believers, we are to be aware of our thought processes. Just because a thought enters into your mind, that does not mean that thought *originated* in your mind. It may have originated in the mind of a demon that then placed that trumped-up thought into your mind. A demon's hope is that you will accept the thought as though it had originated from within your own mind. When the demon manipulates your emotions and you react with some negative emotion like anger, hate, indifference, or rebellion, you are set up. Demons expect you to believe that what you are thinking and feeling is factual. Next comes the critical part. If you exercise your will and act upon that faulty information, it is as though you have joined forces with the demon to help him accomplish his nefarious scheme.[66]

David's enemies had made him dwell in dark places where he had no spiritual light. The only way the enemy can make a person dwell in dark places is if God allows it. In that case, He has a purpose behind it for our good. David said his spirit was overwhelmed because of the persecution of his enemies. Their persecution was directed at David's soul—his mind, his emotions, and his will. The enemy's oppressive actions had weighed heavily upon David's mind and emotions. His will did not know which way to turn. The word *overwhelmed* is defined as meaning "to overpower in thought or feeling."[67] David's spirit was feeling feeble and weak. He was lacking courage. He was in a state of despair, and he felt overpowered.

When demonic forces do this to believers, they are oppressed. David was in this condition because the enemy had persecuted his soul. David's heartfelt statement was written in the present tense. My spirit *is* overwhelmed.

David said, "My heart is appalled." He was saying that his understanding was desolate, stunned, or stupefied. It was groggy, and nothing made sense. His mind could not understand what was going on. He was saying that he had no comfort, no cheerfulness, and no hope. Perhaps we might be able to relate to how David felt when we remember our own emotions as the world watched the Twin Towers in New York City fall because of an enemy's unprecedented attack.

Because the enemy had persecuted his soul, David had gotten off track and was not dwelling in the shelter of the Most High. However, once David recognized his condition, he took immediate action and did something about it. Psalm 143 continues,

> I remember the days of old; I meditate on all Your doings; I muse on the work of Your hands. (Psalm 143:5)

What does he do about his condition? David said, "I remember the days of old." Remembering is a function of the mind. When we remember something, we bring something to mind that has happened, and we think about it again. It is bringing to mind something of the past. We think of former times—as contrasted to the present situation. David remembered what God had done in his life. To *meditate* "implies a definite focusing of one's thoughts on something so as to understand it deeply."[68] When we seriously meditate on something, we concentrate on it for an extended period. What we focus our thoughts on should be pleasing to the Lord. David meditated on God's doings. He meditated on His works, His deeds, and His acts.

David mused. To *muse* means "to become absorbed in thought; especially: to think about something carefully and thoroughly."[69] When we *muse*, we become absorbed in thought. We study the issue at hand and ponder it in our mind.

The enemy had attacked David, and his spirit was overwhelmed within him. The enemy's assault against David was a carryover of the same tactic that Lucifer used in the garden of Eden against Eve when he tempted her to ponder what had been deceptively spoken against God.

How did David respond to the attack of the enemy? He began thinking about all that God had done for him in the past. He remembered the good times, and He pondered how God had worked in his life. What was the result? David lifted up his soul to God and began moving in a different direction. Instead of dwelling from his soul, he saw the LORD as trustworthy. He wanted to walk in the ways of the LORD and took refuge in Him.

This should tell us something about our spiritual enemies and how they work. Demons also want us to focus our thoughts on the past. Conversely, they want us to remember past hurts and rejections, and they are quick to prod our memory. They want us to forget what we should remember and to remember what we should forget. They want us to concentrate on the times we felt like God had not come through for us. They may even invent thoughts that are foreign to our way of thinking. They will readily give thoughts that are against God and what He is doing in our life. Then they will try to make us feel guilty for having such horrible thoughts. They want us to feel overwhelmed. They do not want us to understand why things are as they are.

It has been said that what we think about will determine how we feel. When we experience troubling times, do our minds dwell on the works of God, or do they dwell on our perplexing situation? David continued to pour out his heart.

> I stretch out my hands to You; my soul longs for You, as a parched land. Selah. (Psalm 143:6)

When young children stretch out their hands toward an adult, they are looking for comfort, help, or understanding. David, too, was seeking relief and made his requests known to God.

> Answer me quickly, O LORD, my spirit fails; Do not hide Your face from me, Or I will become like those who go down to the pit. Let me hear Your lovingkindness in the morning; For I trust in You; Teach me the way in which I should walk; For to You I lift up my soul. Deliver me, O LORD, from my enemies; I take refuge in You. Teach me to do Your will, For You are my God; Let Your good Spirit lead me on level ground. For the sake of Your name, O LORD, revive me. In Your righteousness bring my soul out of trouble. And in Your lovingkindness, cut off my enemies And destroy all those who afflict my soul, For I am Your servant. (Psalm 143:7–12)

Our spiritual enemies have been given access to us. God is not going to destroy them when they come to oppress. Jesus was aware of that and requested that His Father keep us from the evil one.[70] He does that by sanctifying us in the truth.[71] When we are armed with God's truth, we are able to stand firm against the schemes of the devil,[72] and we have the ability to extinguish his flaming missiles.[73]

The Lord does strengthen and protect us from the evil one.[74] However, if God took care of the evil one by Himself, there would be no need to strengthen us at all. Thankfully, He does set limits on what the demonic forces can do to us.

We are admonished to learn to overcome the evil one while we are young.[75] Would it be wise to instruct our children in the ways the enemy works and teach them to understand the issues of spiritual warfare early in life? Many believers I counsel often complain about how they were not taught the issues concerning spiritual warfare either in their youth or as adults. Because of their lack of knowledge, they learn that oftentimes they have suffered needlessly at the hand of their spiritual enemies. Then they frequently ask a very appropriate but perplexing question, "Why have we not been taught these things before?"

The prophet Hosea declared that the people of God are destroyed because of their lack of knowledge. In reality, all Christians should be taught the truth concerning the tactics our spiritual enemies use against us and how we can be overwhelmingly victorious in our opposition against them. Sadly, that is often the exception rather than the rule. Although the enemy purposed to persecute David's soul and put him in a dark place, God allowed it for David's good. In his despair the psalmist makes a number of vows to God. David said, "I trust in You; for to You I lift up my soul." In essence, he is saying, "Here is my soul. Do with it as You will." He said, "I take refuge in You." By making such a statement, David declared that he would trust in God and in no other person or thing. He declared, "You are my God." In other words, he was saying, "I serve You, not myself or any other thing." David stepped a little further out on the limb when he said, "I am Your servant." He was declaring his willingness to do anything that God might ask of him!

- **Learning to Trust God**

Those who dwell in the shelter of the Most High have declared the LORD to be their refuge and fortress. God may create situations to stir up and force would-be dwellers out of their comfort zones.

He provides hands-on instruction and teaches us to honestly trust God. In Deuteronomy, the King James Version of the Bible gives us an interesting example from an eagle's perspective.

> As an eagle stirreth up her nest, fluttereth over her young, spreadeth abroad her wings, taketh them, beareth them on her wings. (Deuteronomy 32:11 KJV)

We see a graphic picture of this as we observe a mother eagle teaching her young eaglets to fly.

> The eagle is known for its ferocity, yet no member of the bird family is more gentle and attentive to its young. At just the right time, the mother eagle begins to teach her eaglets how to fly. She gathers an eaglet onto her back and, spreading her wings, flies high. Suddenly she swoops out from under the eaglet and as it falls, it gradually learns what its wings are for until the mother catches it once again on her wings. Sometimes, the eaglet learns on the first try, but if not, the process is repeated many times. If the young is slow to learn or cowardly she returns him to the nest, and begins to tear her nest apart, until there is nothing left for the eaglet to cling to. Then she nudges him off the cliff. Those in Christ learn to depend on the faithful Father, knowing that underneath are His arms ready to bear His children up, to support and carry them through all of life's storms.[76]

By nudging the eaglet off the cliff, the mother eagle is forcing the immature eaglet into a situation that will help persuade it to live according to its nature. Although immature and unwilling to fly, the eaglet's nature, its bent, is to fly and soar like an eagle.

As we learn to dwell in the shelter of the Most High, God carries us for a while, and then it seems as though He drops us. We may flounder as we try to make sense of our downward, spiraling situation. Because we are weak and have not yet learned to effectively use our spiritual wings, God soon undergirds us and lifts us up. The process continues until we gain confident strength and learn to live as though the Lord actually was our refuge and fortress. If we are reluctant to step out in faith, God may begin removing all that we cling to that would prevent us from fully trusting Him. Isaiah 40 adds an encouraging word.

> Yet those who wait for the LORD Will gain new strength; They will mount up with wings like eagles, They will run and not get tired, They will walk and not become weary. (Isaiah 40:31)

How does a person learn to trust God? Although people can easily speak words declaring their trust in God, their actions do not always make the same declaration. In Luke 6, Jesus said,

> "And why do you call Me, 'Lord, Lord,' and do not do what I say?" (Luke 6:46)

The words spoken by those the Lord addressed declared that Jesus was their Lord. However, their actions spoke volumes about what they actually believed in their heart.

The story is told of a man pushing a wheelbarrow on a cable that had been stretched across Niagara Falls. Upon his safe return from the far side of the falls, the man asked the quickly gathering crowd if they thought he could do it again. They had seen him accomplish the round-trip task once, so they figured he could do it again, and he did. Upon his next successful return, the man pushing the wheelbarrow asked his original question to a nearby student who had been thoughtfully observing. Once the student answered the question in the affirmative, the wheelbarrow-pushing man—who was poised to launch another adventure across the cable—quietly invited the student to get into the wheelbarrow.

It would be one thing to agree that the man pushing the wheelbarrow *could* make another successful round trip on the cable. However, it might be a very different thing to trust him enough to get into the wheelbarrow!

So how could Christians learn to trust God? God offers us various opportunities to climb into His precariously perched wheelbarrow! It is one thing to declare that God is capable of doing something. It may be quite a different issue to trust Him in the process.

The book of James makes this revealing pronouncement:

> But wilt thou know, O vain man, that faith without works is dead? (James 2:20 KJV)

Once we learn to trust God in the wheelbarrow encounters of life, we will have a valid confidence in our Creator. We have learned to trust God not only in reference to our vocational work but also in the responsibilities that come to us throughout our life. We can trust Him as we go through various trials that come our way. Even more, we will trust Him with our dreams and hopes for the future. We can speak with assurance because our reliance is upon God alone. We have found the object of our trust to be trustworthy.

Such is the case for the man of Psalm 91:2. He has made a vow to God and made his bold affirmation, "I will say to the LORD, my refuge and my fortress, my God, in whom I trust!" Once we make such a declaration, it will not be long before our invitation to climb into God's wheelbarrow confronts us. When we make such a declaration to the Lord, we are speaking to the One who judges righteously. Therefore, He tests our words to see what is in our hearts by providing trials in life to determine if we truly trust Him. Our decision will reveal our heart.

If we make a vow to our righteous judge and declare that He is our refuge, He will keep working and maturing us until He has our dross removed. He will allow us to encounter various situations that will test whether or not He truly is our refuge … or if our words amount to lip service only. For example, we know that God wants us to pay our tithe. If the car breaks down and we use our tithe to have it repaired, we rob God. Our heart reveals our lack of trust that God will supply our needs. However, what God allows, He allows for our good. When these adverse circumstances come our way, we usually react with a less than godly attitude—regardless of the message from the book of James.

> Consider it all joy, my brethren, when you encounter various trials, knowing that the testing of your faith produces endurance. And let endurance have its perfect result, that you may be perfect and complete, lacking in nothing. (James 1:2–4)

We should have the same attitude toward the various trials that we encounter when we go to a trusted dentist. We may not enjoy the time when the dentist is actually doing the work of drilling and probing, but we know it is for our well-being. During the various trials that God allows in our life, we need to consider it all joy because the God of the Universe is at work and is moving us in the direction of spiritual maturity. James adds these wise statements:

> For we all stumble in many ways. If anyone does not stumble in what he says, he is a perfect man, able to bridle the whole body as well. (James 3:2)

> So also the tongue is a small part of the body, and yet it boasts of great things. Behold, how great a forest is set aflame by such a small fire! (James 3:5)

> But no one can tame the tongue; it is a restless evil and full of deadly poison. (James 3:8)

The tongue cannot be tamed because what it speaks comes from the heart.[77] If we do not stumble in the words of our Psalm 91:2 declaration, we will find ourselves in the shelter of the Most High, abiding in the shadow of the Almighty!

We will begin to see why the man of verse 2 has this confidence and trust in Elohim in the next verse.

Summary

I will say to the LORD, "My refuge and my fortress,
my God, in whom I trust!"

In this verse, we found two more names for God—Jehovah and Elohim. The Hebrew word *Jehovah* is written in English as "LORD" in most translations and means the active, self-existent One. The Hebrew word for *Elohim* is written as "God" in most translations and means "the strong faithful One—the only true God." We also glanced at what it means to trust God through a lesson from David's experience found in Psalm 143. Learning to trust God was likened to an eagle teaching her eaglets to fly and to God's wheelbarrow encounters of life.

Psalm 91:3

It Is He Who Delivers You

**For it is He who delivers you from the snare of
the trapper, And from the deadly pestilence.**

God has potentially delivered the inhabitants of the world from
the original snare of the trapper by sending the Lord Jesus Christ
to die for our sins. I say *potentially* because God's gift must be
received in order to be possessed. All have fallen victim to Satan's
original snare, and as a result, we have been separated from God.

The word *deliver* means "to snatch away, rescue, to save."[78]
Once we are saved, we are delivered from Satan's kingdom. We are
not involved in that decision. It is automatic and has been put into
place by our Creator. Colossians 1 tells us about that deliverance.

> For He delivered us from the domain of darkness,
> and transferred us to the kingdom of His beloved
> Son, in whom we have redemption, the forgiveness
> of sins. (Colossians 1:13–14)

Deliverance from the domain of darkness has already been
accomplished for every believer through the Lord Jesus Christ.
True Christians have been automatically and legally transferred
out of the jurisdiction of the kingdom of darkness and immediately

placed under the jurisdiction of Christ. Our title of ownership has been transferred to our new proprietor. Therefore, Christians are no longer under the domain, authority, or jurisdiction of their previous owner.

For it is He who delivers you ... The "you" refers to the one who has learned to dwell in the shelter of the Most High. Dwellers have learned to trust God even when their understanding and logic seem to be operating in the dark. This deliverance occurs while we are yet on earth. It cannot be referring to some future time when we are in heaven because there will be no trapper in heaven. It pertains to our time on earth as we dwell in the shelter of the Most High.

For it is He who delivers you
from the snare of the trapper ...

A snare is something by which one is entangled or impeded like when a net is thrown over an animal or a bird. The entrapped creature does not even recognize the snare before it is caught. Once it has been caught, it is too late to avoid the trap and will thereby suffer the consequences. A trapper lays out bait in a trap.

Although believers have been transferred out of the domain of darkness at the point of salvation, the enemy can still ensnare us. The followers of Christ live in a different kingdom than unbelievers and have been given the authority and power to overcome their spiritual enemies. Unfortunately, not all Christians utilize their God-given authority and power. Our verse at hand tells us that God delivers the one who dwells in the shelter of the Most High from the enemy's snare. The Treasury of David offers insight on this verse.

> Assuredly no subtle plot shall succeed against one
> who has the eyes of God watching for his defence.
> We are foolish and weak as poor little birds, and are
> very apt to be lured to our destruction by cunning
> foes, but if we dwell near to God, he will see to it
> that the most skillful deceiver shall not entrap us.

> "Satan the fowler who betrays
> Unguarded souls a thousand ways,"

shall be foiled in the case of the man whose high and honourable condition consists in residence within the holy place of the Most High.[79]

If God delivers us from the snare of the trapper, why should believers concern themselves with spiritual warfare? James informs us that God's deliverance from the snares of our enemies is not automatic.

> Submit therefore to God. Resist the devil and he will flee from you. (James 4:7)

We must do our part. As would-be dwellers, we must choose to operate from our spirit to engage the enemy in spiritual warfare. From the position of experiencing the Lord as our refuge and fortress as we submit to God and put our trust in Him, God will deliver us from the snare of the trapper. If believers were automatically delivered from the snare of the trapper as an act of God, there would be no need for personal spiritual warfare.

Here are a few ways God has provided to deliver believers from the snare of the trapper.

1. God sets limits on what the enemy can do. For example, God set limits on Satan when he first aspired to attack Job. God gave him permission to touch Job's possessions but would not allow Satan to touch Job's body. Second, God forbade Satan to take Job's life.[80] If Satan and the kingdom of darkness could do whatever they wanted to the people of God unhindered by God's restraint, they would kill us all.

2. Jesus utilized on-the-job training to teach His disciples hand-to-hand combat with the enemy. The disciples had attempted to cast a demon out of a lad but were unsuccessful. When Jesus came on the scene, He rebuked the demon, and it left. The disciples wanted to know why they were not able to cast

it out. Jesus told them it was because of their lack of faith.[81] Jesus used their own failure to increase their knowledge. As we read and study Scripture, we can put what we learn into practice any time we find ourselves confronting the world, the flesh, or the kingdom of darkness.

3. God enables believers today to engage in meaningful spiritual warfare by providing us with the necessary authority and power needed to overcome demonic forces.[82] Without that authority and power, we would have no recourse against our spiritual enemies.

4. God equips us with His armor whereby we can safely engage the enemy in successful warfare.[83] We do not use the armor of God to deliver us from the *domain* of the kingdom of darkness. Salvation effectively does that. If a Christian does not know what the armor is—or know how to put it on—that Christian is in no condition to engage in effective spiritual warfare.

5. God gives us His Word and His Spirit. We must use them to evaluate what we hear from others. After Jesus had informed His disciples that He would be going to Jerusalem and would be killed, Peter took Jesus aside and rebuked Him. Peter assured Him that such a thing would not happen on his shift. Jesus said that Peter was a stumbling block to Him. Peter had not evaluated the thoughts that were freely roaming around in his mind. Rather he engaged those thoughts, allowed his emotions to get involved, and then offered advice to his Lord that had come from Satan. Peter had become trapped in Satan's snare.

Dwellers are assured that they will be delivered from the snare of the trapper. Psalm 124 provides hope.

> Our soul has escaped as a bird out of the snare of the trapper; The snare is broken and we have escaped. (Psalm 124:7)

**For it is He who delivers you from the snare of
the trapper, *And from the deadly pestilence.***

If something is deadly, it is likely to cause or produce death.
In a sense, Satan's original snare in the garden of Eden was
potentially deadly. Once the snare was laid, Eve was deceived,
and the choice was made to act upon the serpent's temptation.
That decision, embraced by both Adam and Eve, brought death
to their fellowship with God because He said, "From any tree of
the garden you may eat freely; but from the tree of the knowledge
of good and evil you shall not eat, for in the day that you eat from
it you will surely die." The serpent provided the temptation, but
the choice was theirs.

Satan did not bring death to Adam and Eve's fellowship with
God. Satan does not have that much authority or power. Satan's
snare didn't *cause* them to be driven from the garden of Eden
either. If Satan had that much authority and power, he would not
be that obliging. In other words if he could, he would have caused
them to disobey God so that they would be separated from Him
just as he was. Again, he does not have that kind of authority or
power.

Psalm 91:3 tells us that this pestilence is deadly. A deadly
pestilence produces death. Although it was Satan's desire that
humanity would be forever separated from God, Satan's garden
snare did not place a deadly pestilence upon humanity. Apparently,
Satan knew what God had said to Adam. How else would he have
known they were not to eat from the Tree of the Knowledge of
Good and Evil? Based on his experience Satan knew if he could
tempt the couple to disobey God and rebel, they would be ousted
from the garden just as he had been ousted from his former
place of prominence. However, he knew nothing of God's plan
of salvation!

Satan provides us with temptations aplenty, but God brings on
pestilence when His people sin against Him.[84] Although Satan's
various temptations provide the opportunity, God has promised

to loose the pestilence because of our fleshly, worldly actions. The pestilence then provides an encouragement to repent and turn from our wicked ways. Once the choice to repent is carried out, God forgives and lifts the plague. We cannot dwell in the shelter of the Most High unless we have confessed our sin.

Summary

For it is He who delivers you from the snare of the trapper, And from the deadly pestilence.

In this chapter, we saw that God delivers every Christian from the *domain* of the trapper, but He delivers the dweller from the *snare* of the trapper. The trapper laid a snare for Adam and Eve in the garden of Eden. Their falling into the snare has affected the whole of the human race to this very day. Although Satan's power is restricted, his temptations are designed to provide an opportunity to sin against the God we love.

Although the kingdom of darkness may bring temptations our way, God brings on a deadly pestilence when His people sin against Him.

Psalm 91:4

He Will Cover You

He will cover you with His pinions, And under His wings you may seek refuge; His faithfulness is a shield and bulwark.

Christians need to be covered because we are vulnerable to fleshly, worldly, and spiritual forces that intend to harm us. Their purposes are designed to neutralize or destroy us. Referring to the dweller, this verse emphatically states that God will cover you.

In times of need or prosperity, God has us covered. That is why we can run to Him and seek refuge. As God covers and protects us, nothing can get to us unless it passes through Him first. Such was the case with Job. Without God's explicit permission, all the father of lies could do with Job was to observe how good God had been to him. God had placed a hedge about Job that the would-be antagonist found impossible to penetrate. The evil one had formed an opinion about Job and expounded his theory to God. God partially removed His hedge and allowed Satan to test his theory. In the process, God used Satan's efforts as a springboard to purge Job of unwanted spiritual dross. In the end, Job and his friends had a better understanding of God, and Satan's theory was proven inaccurate. Everything that Satan had stolen from Job was restored twofold. God had Job covered.

He will cover you *with His pinions ...*

The word *pinions* refers to feathers. Many have told the story of a prairie chicken that had been through a forest fire with her chicks. The fire had surrounded them and left no way out. The chicks were too young to fly, so the hen spread her wings and gave the chicks a place where they could seek protection. When the firefighters came upon the scene, they discovered that the fire had killed the hen, but the chicks were still alive underneath her protective wings. Obviously, God does not have feathers, and of course, the fire would not affect Him. Nevertheless, the verse does give a vivid word picture and reveals that God spreads His protective shield over us in times of danger.

Jesus used the same analogy in Matthew 23 when He said,

> "O Jerusalem, Jerusalem, who kills the prophets and stones those who are sent to her! How often I wanted to gather your children together, the way a hen gathers her chicks under her wings, and you were unwilling." (Matthew 23:37)

In chapter 2 of this book, we were introduced to the procedure a mother eagle uses to teach her eaglets to fly. The figurative language used in the thirty-second chapter of Deuteronomy declares the faithfulness of God.

> "Like an eagle that stirs up its nest, That hovers over its young, He spread His wings and caught them, He carried them on His pinions." (Deuteronomy 32:11)

Here Moses refers to what the LORD had done for the children of Israel while under the iron fist of Pharaoh. Moses likens the actions of the LORD to those of a mother eagle. He stirred up their nest and hovered over them. That is, He allowed the Egyptians to afflict them until they wanted freedom from their oppressors. They wanted out of their uncomfortable nest. Once freed from Egyptian bondage, the LORD carried them like a mother eagle carries her learning eaglets on her wings. He carried them through the wilderness and on into the Promised Land.

In abbreviated form, Exodus 19 provides an accurate summary.

> 'You yourselves have seen what I did to the Egyptians, and how I bore you on eagles' wings, and brought you to Myself.' (Exodus 19:4)

Albert Barnes supplies this commentary:

> Both in the law and in the Gospel, the Church is compared to fledgelings which the mother cherishes and protects under her wings: but in the law that mother is an eagle, in the Gospels "a hen"; thus shadowing forth the diversity of administration under each covenant: the one of power, which God manifested when He brought His people out of Egypt with a mighty hand and an outstretched arm, and led them into the promised land; the other of grace, when Christ came in humility and took the form of a servant and became obedient unto death, even the death of the Cross.[85]

He will cover you with His pinions,
and under His wings you may seek refuge ...

We only need to seek refuge when we are vulnerable to the varied attacks of an enemy. If there were no enemies that intend to besiege us, there would be no need to seek any kind of refuge. Strong's Concordance defines *refuge* as meaning "to flee for protection; figuratively to confide in, have hope, make refuge, trust."[86] Under His wings you shall flee for protection, confide in, have hope, or put your trust in. To get under something's wing, you must be close to it. In order for a prairie chicken's chicks to take advantage of the protection afforded by the hen's wings, the chicks must be close enough to get to that place of safety before danger overtakes and consumes them.

The KJV reads, "And under his wings shalt thou trust." The word translated as *refuge* in the NASB is translated as *trust* in the KJV. We could paraphrase the sentence in this manner: "You can find security beneath God's protective covering when an enemy comes near. You will confide in, have hope in, and make your refuge there. You will put your trust in God's provided protection."

Although this protection is available, it is not automatic. Under His wings, *you may seek* refuge. It must be sought. The mother prairie chicken offered protection to her chicks in the midst of their scorching circumstances.

Although the young chicks had the ability to seek refuge beneath a rock outcropping, a hollowed-out log, or some other source, they sought the protection offered by their mother's outstretched wings. Through God-given instinct, it was natural for the chicks to scurry to their mother's side where they found safety and security.

In like manner, we must make the choice to run to God and seek His refuge instead of taking refuge in our flesh, our own knowledge, our abilities, our understanding, our trust in the world system, our finances, our job, etc. Unfortunately, running to God as our primary refuge is not encouraged by our flesh or by the world. Running to God is not our normal response when faced with undesirable circumstances.

He will cover you with His pinions, And under His wings you may seek refuge; *His faithfulness is a shield and bulwark*.

His faithfulness is a shield. Who needs such a shield and bulwark? Those who are in danger of being assaulted by an enemy that is determined to cause great harm. A shield is something that protects or defends. As a shield, His faithfulness is part of our protective armor. Without question, God is faithful. Moses and Isaiah found God to be faithful. So did Hosea, Paul, the writer to the Hebrews, Peter, and John. They and every other Bible character found God to be faithful, as have believers throughout the world.

His faithfulness is a shield and bulwark. The KJV reads, "His truth shall be thy shield and buckler." The word the NASB uses for faithfulness is translated ninety-two times as *truth* in the Old Testament and only three times is it translated as *faithfully*, *faithful*, or *faithfulness*. According to the KJV, God's truth is a shield for us. In John 8, Jesus said,

> Jesus therefore was saying to those Jews who had believed Him, "If you abide in My word, then you are truly disciples of Mine; and you shall know the truth, and the truth shall make you free." (John 8:31–32)

Those disciples who continue in God's Word will know the truth, and that truth will set them free. The truth sets us free. A lie believed will put us in bondage. The word *believe* is defined as meaning "to consider to be true or honest; to accept the word or evidence of."[87] In other words, if we receive a lie as though it is true and honest and accept it as such, we will find ourselves in bondage to the lie because of the overshadowing of the truth. God's truth is a shield that surrounds and protects dwellers from lies that emanate from the world, the flesh, or our spiritual enemies.

Albert Barnes defines *buckler* (bulwark in the NASB) as follows:

> The word rendered buckler is derived from the verb "to surround" and is given to the defensive armor here referred to, because it "surrounds," and thus "protects" a person.[88]

God is faithful. He has given us His truth. As we continue in His Word as disciples, we will surround ourselves with that truth, which, in turn, will effectively shield us from the lies of our enemies.

Summary

He will cover you with His pinions, And under his wings you may seek refuge; His faithfulness is a shield and bulwark.

God has us covered in good times and in those that are not as favorable. A word picture using a mother prairie chicken was given to illustrate how God spreads His protective shield over us in times of danger. Although not automatic, we have the choice to flee to God for refuge and to put our trust in His provided protection. His faithfulness and truth surround us, shield us, and protect us as we put our trust in Him.

Psalm 91:5

You Will Not Be Afraid
Part 1

You will not be afraid of the terror by night,
Or of the arrow that flies by day;

Psalm 27 provides us with a pertinent reminder.

> Though a host encamp against me, My heart will
> not fear; Though war arise against me, In spite of
> this I shall be confident. (Psalm 27:3)

Fear is defined as "an unpleasant often strong emotion caused by anticipation or awareness of danger."[89] When we are afraid, we are experiencing fear. How could fear give ground for a demon to work? Fear has the same effect with the kingdom of darkness that faith has with God. Fear allows Satan's forces to work in our lives, whereas faith allows God to work in our lives.

Scripture informs us that the knowing of the truth will make us free. The converse is obvious. If we listen to a lie, it will put us in bondage. For example, if oppressed Christians believe that demons cannot influence the life of a true believer, a demon could easily interject fear any time the subject is broached. When fear in such a circumstance registers on our emotions, it is an easy thing to make the choice to avoid such topics at all costs. As a result, the oppressed individual has exchanged the truth of God for a lie. One's reaction to fear gives ground to the demon because the enemy's lie has been heard and accepted.

When you dwell in the shelter of the Most High, you will not experience the emotion of fear that comes from the enemy as he attempts to terrorize you. Instead you will experience a boldness to exercise spiritual authority over the enemy. By doing so, you will force the demonic antagonist to flee from you.

If we are experiencing terror, we are in a state of intense fear. The book of Job gives an example. Eliphaz, one of Job's counselors, told Job of a spiritual intruder he had encountered. This intruder was a spirit that had intentionally come to oppress Eliphaz while he was sleeping. The encounter caused him to experience such monumental fear and dread that his body began to tremble and shake.[90]

It is well known that darkness can bring out intense fear that is not present during daylight hours. For instance, a walk in the woods during hours of daylight will not create the fear or dread that might be felt on the same walk during the nighttime hours. In spiritual darkness, the probability of experiencing fear or terror is greatly increased.

Many believers have not been sufficiently taught to recognize when they are being oppressed by a demon. Demonic oppression frequently occurs during the nighttime hours and commonly brings fear and/or dread with it. However, oppression in the night is no problem for those dwelling in the shelter of the Most High because they know how to utilize spiritual warfare to effectively take authority over the enemy.

You will not be afraid of the terror by night,
Or of the arrow that flies by day;

What is the arrow that flies by day? Psalm 11 says,

For, behold, the wicked bend the bow, They make ready their arrow upon the string, To shoot in darkness at the upright in heart. (Psalm 11:2)

Demonic forces want to shoot their arrows at the upright in heart during a period of darkness. There are two words contained in Psalm 11:2 that also appear in verses 5 and 6 of Psalm 91, specifically *arrow* and *darkness*. When we examine Psalm 91:6, we will find a deeper meaning to the word *darkness*.

Although demons do harass people in the daytime, they frequently come in the night while people are sleeping. Either way, they launch their poisonous arrows in the form of contaminated thoughts that they place in a person's mind. Unsuspecting Christians will think those are their own thoughts and may be very disturbed that such thoughts are roaming about freely in the mind. Hating the invading thoughts, the child of God may attempt to take them captive only to discover the thoughts keep returning with a vile vengeance.

As we will see later in the psalm, dwellers have learned how to recognize and take authority over demonic forces. Additionally, they have learned how to neutralize their enemies' ill-intentioned arrows. Although the arrows may come from a family member, friend, neighbor, or coworker in the form of hurtful words that cut like a sword,[91] they do not alarm dwellers. They simply deal with them on a spiritual level and go on with life.

There are times, however, when people may have a subtle, enemy-inspired thought that is seemingly innocuous and that many believe comes from God. For example, a woman told me that as she was riding down a two-lane country road with her husband, she had the thought he would run over a squirrel. Although she had said nothing to her husband, within minutes a squirrel dashed out right in front of their car, and they ran over it.

On another occasion the same woman told me that she had had a premonition that her teenage son would wet the bed that night. She dismissed the thought because he had not done that for years. Nevertheless, by morning her son's wet bed provided credibility that the thought had indeed been accurate. Therefore, she assumed the thought must have originated from God.

One day the woman was getting ready to work in her yard. A thought crossed her mind that she would soon experience pain in her back. She dismissed the thought because her back had not been bothering her at all. Shortly after going outside, however, she felt a twinge of pain in her back that soon began escalating in intensity. She was bewildered and began thinking about the other thoughts she had had. She wondered why God would bother to inform her of such trivial matters. She remembered learning that demons could put thoughts into a person's mind and decided to treat the pain in her back as one of the enemy's arrows. When she did, the pain vanished as quickly as it had arrived. She discovered that God had not given the thoughts. The bogus thoughts were a subtle device of the enemy trying to gain access to her mind and to her body. Ephesians 6 says,

> In addition to all, taking up the shield of faith with which you will be able to extinguish all the flaming arrows of the evil one. (Ephesians 6:16)

These arrows are the contaminated thoughts that come from the enemy. Dwellers will not be afraid of the terror that the enemy brings, and the enemy's flaming arrows won't damage them. This verse does not say the terror or the arrows will not come. However, when they do come, they will not have the affect they once had in our lives.

As we dwell in the shelter of the Most High and abide in the shadow of the Almighty, dwellers will not be afraid because God is our refuge and our fortress. A person cannot dwell in the shelter of the Most High if he or she believes and accepts a lie from the enemy.[92]

Have you ever experienced a demonic intruder unleashing fear or terror upon you or one of your children in the night? Can you imagine how people might feel if they had a nighttime visitation from a demon and did not know what it was or how to deal with it? That could develop into a very frightening situation.[93]

Our enemies can influence our minds with their insidious arrows, but they can also influence our emotions with their fears.

Summary

**You will not be afraid of the terror by night,
Or of the arrow that flies by day;**

Fear is often an unpleasant and strong emotion caused by the anticipation or awareness of danger. Instead of experiencing nighttime fear or terror from spiritual enemies, dwellers are not alarmed. Dwellers not only learn to recognize and reject the enemies' arrows that come in the form of subtle thoughts directed into the mind or fear-induced feelings directed at the emotions, but they have learned to exercise God-given authority over their spiritual antagonists and have forced them to flee.

Notes

Psalm 91:6

You Will Not Be Afraid
Part 2

**You will not be afraid of the terror by night,
Or of the arrow that flies by day;**

(You will not be afraid)
Of the pestilence that stalks in darkness,

You will not be afraid … of the pestilence. It is interesting that the psalmist has already used the word *pestilence* at the end of verse 3. Why would he bring it up and use the same word again? The pestilence mentioned in verse 3 refers to something God brings upon His people because they are disobedient. For instance, in the book of Deuteronomy, God told the children of Israel the outcome should they choose to disobey.

> "The LORD will make the pestilence cling to you
> until He has consumed you from the land, where
> you are entering to possess it." (Deuteronomy 28:21)

The word *pestilence* is used in thirty-eight Old Testament verses in the NASB. Each time it references something that God brings upon the disobedient. In Psalm 91:6, however, the pestilence "stalks." The pestilence is doing the stalking. What or whom does the pestilence stalk? A look at verses 5 and 6 will help make that determination.

You will not be afraid of the terror by night, or of the arrow that flies by day; of the pestilence that stalks in darkness, or of the destruction that lays waste at noon. (Psalm 91:5–6)

What or whom is being stalked? The man of Psalm 91 is being stalked. It may be of interest to note that when God brings pestilence, people are warned beforehand. God's pestilence does not stalk. It strikes as foretold. We find an example of this when Moses talked to Pharaoh about allowing the children of Israel to leave Egypt so they could serve the LORD. Moses's warning is found in the book of Exodus.

Then the LORD said to Moses, "Go to Pharaoh and speak to him, 'Thus says the LORD, the God of the Hebrews, "Let My people go, that they may serve Me. For if you refuse to let them go, and continue to hold them, behold, the hand of the LORD will come with a very severe pestilence on your livestock which are in the field, on the horses, on the donkeys, on the camels, on the herds, and on the flocks. But the LORD will make a distinction between the livestock of Israel and the livestock of Egypt, so that nothing will die of all that belongs to the sons of Israel."'" (Exodus 9:1–4)

If you were to read the rest of the story, you would find that the LORD had even set a definite time for the pestilence to strike. Through Moses, He told Pharaoh it would come upon them the next day, and it did. As foretold, the livestock of Egypt died.

The word *stalk* is defined as meaning "to go through an area in search of prey or quarry."[94] For example, we could say that hunters would stalk through the woods in search of their prey. Have you ever witnessed a cat stalking a bird? The cat will stealthily sneak up on the unsuspecting bird as it walks slowly, determinedly, and cautiously with the intent of capturing the prey. The cat is in *stalk* mode.

The pestilence spoken of in this verse stalks in the darkness. The word *darkness* is defined as darkness, gloom, spiritual unreceptivity, and calamity.[95] When we are not receptive to spiritual things, it could be said that we are in the dark. Of the nine times this Hebrew word for darkness is used, six of those uses are found in the book of Job, and it is used once in Psalm 91:6, as we have already seen.

The tenth chapter of the book of Job is the outcry of a man in a dark gloom. Listen to Job as he emotionally vents his thoughts.

"I loathe my own life; I will give full vent to my complaint; I will speak in the bitterness of my soul. I will say to God, 'Do not condemn me; Let me know why You contend with me. Is it right for You indeed to oppress, To reject the labor of Your hands, And to look favorably on the schemes of the wicked? Have You eyes of flesh? Or do You see as a man sees? Are Your days as the days of a mortal, Or Your years as man's years, That You should seek for my guilt And search after my sin? According to Your knowledge I am indeed not guilty, Yet there is no deliverance from Your hand. Your hands fashioned and made me altogether, And would You destroy me? Remember now, that You have made me as clay; And would You turn me into dust again? Did You not pour me out like milk And curdle me like cheese; Clothe me with skin and flesh, And knit me together with bones and sinews? You have granted me life and lovingkindness; And Your care has preserved my spirit. Yet these things You have concealed in Your heart; I know that this is within You: If I sin, then You would take note of me, And would not acquit me of my guilt. If I am wicked, woe to me! And if I am righteous, I dare not lift up my head. *I am* sated with disgrace and conscious of my misery. Should *my head* be lifted up, You would hunt me like a lion;

And again You would show Your power against me. You renew Your witnesses against me And increase Your anger toward me; Hardship after hardship is with me. Why then have You brought me out of the womb? Would that I had died and no eye had seen me! I should have been as though I had not been, Carried from womb to tomb.' "Would He not let my few days alone? Withdraw from me that I may have a little cheer Before I go—and I shall not return—To the land of darkness and deep shadow, The land of utter gloom as darkness *itself,* Of deep shadow without order, And which shines as the darkness." (Job 10:1–22)

Would you think that Job was in the dark and spiritually unreceptive at the time? Was not his mood one of deep gloom?

The pestilence that stalks in the darkness comes from our spiritual enemies. Oppressing demons can definitely cause their own form of affliction or pestilence. The sixth verse of Psalm 91 does not say or even suggest that pestilence will not come to us. Remembering that any pestilence from God coming upon the disobedient is a fearful thing, we are informed in this verse that the dweller will not be afraid of the pestilence. That is true because this pestilence is not from the hand of God. Although it is from our spiritual enemies, we have authority over them and need not fear what they try to bring upon us.

Demons have the ability to afflict us by oppressing our soul— our mind, emotions, and will—as they give feelings of depression, fear, anxiety, dread, anger, hate, rebellion, rejection, etc. When a demon oppresses a person's body, it can do so by causing a headache or a feeling of emotional or physical heaviness. Demons can also cause a person to feel sick, to shake, or to experience bodily pain. We know that Satan gave Job boils over his entire body.[96] Doctor Luke informed us that a woman had been plagued by a sickness for eighteen years and that it had been caused by a spirit.[97] In reference to the last plague that overwhelmed Pharaoh, God used a band of evil, destroying angels to bring death to the Egyptians' firstborn children.[98]

A woman was scheduled to come in for an appointment but was physically feeling quite ill. She was so ill that she asked her friend who was planning to attend the session with her to cancel the appointment. When her friend called to cancel the appointment, it was suggested they make use of the spiritual warfare they had learned to see if that brought any change in the counselee's illness. They followed the advice they had been given, and instantly, the afflicted woman felt normal and was able to keep her appointment. A spiritual enemy had afflicted her.

Aware of it or not, like it or not, demons can definitely afflict a Christian's soul and body. Dwellers would not fear the pestilence brought on by demonic forces. They know they have access to the shelter of the Most High, and dwellers know how to use their God-given authority against their demonic antagonists. Dwellers are also open and ready to receive and use whatever spiritual warfare tactics the Holy Spirit teaches them.

The word *stalk* is also defined as meaning "to pursue obsessively and to the point of harassment."[99] God's pestilence is not designed to harass us. It is designed to bring us back into fellowship with Him. Since Satan's most cherished desire was to be like the Most High, he imitates what God does. The god of this world is a counterfeiter. As such, his kingdom offers its own brand of pestilence. Like a cat stalking a bird, a demon will stalk us, watch us, and wait for an opportune moment to attack.

The pestilence mentioned in this verse stalks in darkness. If a place is filled with darkness, there is little or no light. In the demonic realm, darkness is the state of being unenlightened spiritually. Demons attack those areas of our lives in which we have little or no spiritual understanding. If believed, an enemy's deceptions will put a person in a state of spiritual darkness or spiritual blindness.[100] The enemy's stalking is meant to produce pestilence in our lives and to put us in the dark spiritually. Demons can make a person dwell in a dark place when the demons' lies are believed. Any time demons make us dwell in dark places, we are there because they have deceived us mentally and thus usher us into the dark. As we believe the enemies' lies, we are aligned with the kingdom of darkness, are eating at the table of demons, and therefore cannot partake of the table of the Lord.[101] That is why demons want to keep a believer in the dark concerning scriptural truth.

You will not be afraid of the pestilence that stalks in darkness, *Or of the destruction that lays waste at noon.*

The word *destruction* means "to cut off; ruin, destroying."[102] When God has us in a dark place, He intends to bring destruction to our fleshly or worldly ways. Demons want to bring destruction to our godly, spiritual ways. Not only do demons want us to walk after the world and after the flesh, but they also want us to listen to and accept their lies. By even passively listening, we grant demons permission to carry out their evil deeds against us. Demons want to bring destruction to our lives any way they can. Psalm 38 says,

> Those who seek my life lay snares for me; And those who seek to injure me have threatened destruction, And they devise treachery all day long. (Psalm 38:12)

The kingdom of darkness has a despicable purpose—to steal, kill, and destroy. Our spiritual enemies lay snares, seek to injure us, threaten us with destruction, and utilize treachery against us. To *lay waste* means "to deal violently with, despoil, devastate, ruin, destroy, spoil."[103] Is that not reason enough to be on the alert for our spiritual enemies? Demons not only work in the dark, but they can launch their form of pestilence at any time. At noon we are usually in the middle of our daily business. It is a time we may least expect trouble. Since we are in a spiritual war, however, we need to be vigilant at all times.

We can illustrate the reality of Psalm 91:5–6 as we examine the third chapter of the book of Genesis. Psalm 91:5 sets the scene by revealing the arrow that had been loosed by the enemy.

- **The Enemy's Arrow**

> Now the serpent was more crafty than any beast of the field which the LORD God had made. And he said to the woman, "Indeed, has God said, 'You shall not eat from any tree of the garden'?" (Genesis 3:1)

This is the first mention of the serpent in Scripture. Note that God did nothing to prevent the serpent's speaking to Eve. God had already given Adam the truth concerning the Tree of the Knowledge of Good and Evil. Had the newlyweds obeyed God, the serpent would have had no ground on which to work.

Before the crafty creature had spoken a word, a plan had been devised in an attempt to cause the woman to disobey God. The first words out of the serpent's mouth flew like an arrow into Eve's mind and interjected the element of doubt into the conversation. The serpent's words were not launched in an overpowering manner as though from some sort of wild beast. There is no indication that it was yelling or that the serpent was physically intimidating. Yet it spoke as one having authority that was simply challenging God's command. "Indeed, has God said …" The serpent's words were not constructed as a statement of fact but rather as a question that demanded an answer. And Eve had one.

> And the woman said to the serpent, "From the fruit of the trees of the garden we may eat." (Genesis 3:2)

Eve spoke the truth. So far, spiritual accuracy prevailed. However, she went on. The enemy's arrow had found its mark.

- **Spiritual Enemies Bring Pestilence**

> And the woman said to the serpent, "From the fruit
> of the trees of the garden we may eat; but from the
> fruit of the tree which is in the middle of the garden,
> God has said, 'You shall not eat from it or touch it,
> or you will die.'" (Genesis 3:2–3)

Eve related the rest of what God had spoken on the matter but embellished it with three words of her own—"or touch it." When she added her own words to what God had spoken, His statement was modified, and the revision no longer represented the fullness of truth. Thus, she was entrapped. Apparently, she believed what she had spoken was what God had spoken. However, adding to God's truth results in spiritual darkness.

> The serpent said to the woman, "You surely will not
> die!" (Genesis 3:4)

The serpent was no longer simply challenging what God had spoken. Now the crafty creature was openly declaring that God was wrong. On what grounds could such a statement be made? How could it be said that Eve would not die if she ate of the forbidden fruit? Lucifer himself—now operating through the serpent—had disobeyed God yet had not physically died. Therefore, the serpent knew it was speaking truth because he had experienced it firsthand. Did the serpent know that Eve would die spiritually that day? On the other hand, was God's adversary speaking from his own opinion as Eve had done? Upon Lucifer's disobedience, the fallen angel and those that fell with Lucifer were no longer the same as when first created. They were spiritually much different. They had been thrust into total darkness.

In just one sentence, the serpent had spoken the truth and a lie. Looking at the statement from a physical point of view, what had been spoken was true. Eve would not die *physically* on the day she would eat from the forbidden tree. What the serpent failed to convey to Eve was the fact that she would die *spiritually*—just as

God had said. It was Eve's responsibility to respond to the lie based upon the truth that God had given Adam. God had spoken the truth. The day that they would eat from the Tree of the Knowledge of Good and Evil would be the very day they would die. That death would be a spiritual death that would later result in their physical death.[104]

When the serpent spoke, it had lied by telling Eve she would not die that day. Because Eve listened to the serpent, she now had two conflicting pieces of information. God said they would die; the serpent declared that God was wrong. We should be reminded of whom Eve believed every time a woman experiences pain in childbirth[105] or whenever we see a farmer or gardener toiling to produce a crop or garden free of weeds.[106]

Then the serpent provided logic for the statement.

> "For God knows that in the day you eat from it your eyes will be opened, and you will be like God, knowing good and evil." (Genesis 3:5)

Was the serpent speaking truth, sharing its own opinion, or lying again? Scripture does not explain how the serpent gained its information. Nonetheless, what the serpent spoke was true.

> Then the LORD God said, "Behold, the man has become like one of Us, knowing good and evil." (Genesis 3:22)

The serpent told Eve that in eating of the forbidden tree, she would be like God. Should we not all aspire to be more like God? Is it not God's desire that we be conformed into the image of His Son? God's controversy came not because Eve wanted to be like God but the forbidden manner in which she made the attempt.

After hearing the serpent declare that her eyes would be open and that she would be like God, Eve must have taken a long, hard look at the fruit of the forbidden tree. Verse 6 describes the process.

> When the woman saw that the tree was good for
> food, and that it was a delight to the eyes, and that
> the tree was desirable to make one wise, she took
> from its fruit and ate; and she gave also to her
> husband with her, and he ate. (Genesis 3:6)

Here we see the flesh at work. After listening to the serpent's logic, Eve depended upon her own mental and emotional reasoning, and she exercised her will in favor of what the serpent had spoken. She ate of the forbidden fruit, and she shared her bounty with Adam—who was with her. Eve had the ability and the freedom to make her decision, even though it was a bad one—a very bad one!

The serpent was stalking Adam and Eve. His purpose was to bring darkness to the light that God had provided and to plant seeds of spiritual bondage while targeting God's prized creation. In like manner, the kingdom of darkness continues stalking and bringing pestilence to believers today and desires to engulf them in spiritual darkness.

- **Spiritual Enemies Bring Destruction**

You may remember that the word *destruction* means "to cut off; ruin, destroying." We continue the Genesis saga.

> Then the eyes of both of them were opened, and
> they knew that they were naked; and they sewed fig
> leaves together and made themselves loin coverings.
> (Genesis 3:7)

In what ways did the serpent's action and Adam and Eve's decision bring destruction or ruin? The garden's inhabitants experienced shame for the first time in their lives. Previously, they had been naked in the presence of God and each other but had known no shame.[107] The next verse records how they dealt with their newly discovered shame.

> They heard the sound of the LORD God walking
> in the garden in the cool of the day, and the man
> and his wife hid themselves from the presence
> of the LORD God among the trees of the garden.
> (Genesis 3:8)

After eating the forbidden fruit, something had changed. Adam and Eve had a fear of being with God, and they both chose to hide from Him. When God called for Adam, however, the man responded.

> He said, "I heard the sound of Thee in the garden,
> and I was afraid because I was naked; so I hid
> myself." (Genesis 3:10)

Adam must have felt confused. He and his wife had spent time with God in the garden before and had always been naked, but now for the first time, they experienced fear in the presence of God. God did not waste words. He got right to the point.

> And He said, "Who told you that you were naked?
> Have you eaten from the tree of which I commanded
> you not to eat?" (Genesis 3:11)

God had not told them they were naked, and neither had the serpent. They knew they were naked because they had eaten from the proscribed tree and had received the knowledge of good and evil.

God had asked Adam a simple question that could have been answered with one word. Instead Adam assigned blame. He was trying to hold Eve responsible for his own actions.

> The man said, "The woman whom You gave to
> be with me, she gave me from the tree, and I ate."
> (Genesis 3:12)

Nevertheless, Adam's reasoning was faulty. First, he did not acknowledge his sin against God. Second, he avoided taking his responsibility by not taking authority over the serpent as the evil one was conversing with his wife. As a result, Adam chose to listen to the voice of his wife instead of listening and being obedient to the voice of God. God then turned His attention to Eve.

> Then the LORD God said to the woman, "What is this you have done?" And the woman said, "The serpent deceived me, and I ate." (Genesis 3:13)

Eve had become a victim of deception. She had accepted as true or valid that which was false and invalid. Did Adam share any responsibility in Eve being deceived? Yes, he did. Had Adam taken authority over the serpent in the first place, the tempter would not have been around long enough to tempt his wife. Did Eve share any responsibility in being deceived? Yes, she listened to the serpent, and apparently, she believed his argument had merit. Thus, she disregarded what God had spoken and even added a few of her own words to His original proclamation.

Was the serpent the cause of Eve's deception? No, he was not. Although he did provide his own form of pestilence and destruction by way of the temptation, the serpent did not exercise Eve's will. The wily serpent had to allow her to do that.

Because of their sin, God brought judgment upon the garden's inhabitants and drove them from the garden of Eden. Not only had they lost fellowship with God, but the ground was also cursed and began producing thorns and thistles, which has served as a constant reminder and a bane from that day to this—all because Adam listened to the voice of his wife instead of listening to and obeying God.

Summary

You will not be afraid of the terror by night,
Or of the arrow that flies by day;

Of the pestilence that stalks in darkness,
Or of the destruction that lays waste at noon.

As believers, we need to be aware that pestilence, darkness, and destruction can come from our spiritual enemies. Because of the pestilence Satan brought upon Job, the man found himself in a dark gloom, wishing he had never been born. On the other hand, dwellers need not fear the work of the enemy as they dwell in the shelter of the Most High. They are aware of the enemies' tactics and understand how to stand victoriously against them.

Examining Genesis 3:1–13, we saw how the god of this world skillfully loosed his arrow against Adam and Eve in the garden of Eden and brought pestilence and destruction their way. Eve was deceived. She gave the serpent an ear. Because Adam listened to his wife instead of listening to God and obeying Him, He brought judgment upon them and drove them from the garden of Eden. They lost fellowship with God, and the ground bore witness against them by growing thorns and thistles.

Notes

Psalm 91:7

A Thousand May Fall

**A thousand may fall at your side, And ten thousand
at your right hand; But it shall not approach you.**

To understand this verse, we need to understand it from the
context of Psalm 91 and specifically of the two previous verses.

> You will not be afraid of the terror by night, or of the
> arrow that flies by day; of the pestilence that stalks
> in darkness, or of the destruction that lays waste at
> noon. (Psalm 91:5–6)

The word *you* in these two verses is referring to the man of
verse 1—the one who dwells in the shelter of the Most High. He
is the one who will not be afraid of the terror by night, the arrow
that flies by day, the pestilence that stalks in darkness, or the
destruction that lays waste at noon. He is abiding in the shadow
of the Almighty.

In the verse at hand, we are told that a thousand may fall at
your side—at the dweller's side. Are the thousand who are falling
believers or unbelievers? The verse does not specifically say but
does note that they are "at your side." If that refers to them being
alongside you, it could refer to either believers or unbelievers. If "at

your side" means they are *on your side*, they are believers. If the thousand refers to unbelievers, why would only one thousand fall? Why wouldn't all of the unbelievers fall? More likely, the thousand would refer to believers who are falling because unbelievers have no authority or power to fight spiritual enemies. At any rate, one thousand of them fall. However, *only* a thousand fall at your side.

For what reason might the thousand fall? Some may say that the thousand fall because of the pestilence mentioned in Psalm 91:6. Remember, God did not bring on the pestilence mentioned in that verse. That was the work of the enemy.

Neither is the pestilence mentioned in Psalm 91:3 that is brought on by God of concern to dwellers because they are not in rebellion against God. If their fellow believers are affected by God's pestilence, it is because they are in rebellion against Him in some way and would thus have legitimate cause for concern.

A thousand may fall at your side. What does "to fall" mean? The word *fall* can have many uses. One meaning that follows along with the tenor of this entire psalm is found in the book of Leviticus and says,

> But you will chase your enemies, and they will fall
> before you by the sword. (Leviticus 26:7)

A major theme running throughout this psalm involves spiritual warfare. The enemy can entrap Christians who can fall into the reproach and the snare of the devil.[108] When fellow believers stumble, however, they are still "at your side" and "on your side."

In this context, *to fall* means to fall in battle. Why are the thousand falling? They are being defeated in battle. Could *one out of every thousand* be the ratio of Christians who understand and apply spiritual warfare compared to those who do not?

The one thousand fallen ones at your side are being taken captive and falling because they are being defeated in a battle that many do not even know exists. They fall from the terror, the arrow, the pestilence, or various other destructive actions of the enemy. They fall because they do not know that they have a responsibility to engage the enemy in effective spiritual warfare. Hosea summarizes it quite well.

> My people are destroyed for lack of knowledge.
> (Hosea 4:6)

Yet Christians who dwell in the shelter of the Most High can stand in confidence and safety during a spiritual battle. As believers, we are to be more than conquerors,[109] whether we are fighting the world, the flesh, or our spiritual enemies. Our current verse could read like this: "A thousand may fall at your side, and ten thousand may fall at your right hand; however, it shall not approach you."

Because of the sentence structure, whatever happens to the thousand must also happen to the ten thousand. What happens to the thousand? They fall. Therefore, the ten thousand also fall. Leviticus 26 provides some rather interesting statistics.

> But you will chase your enemies, and they will fall before you by the sword; five of you will chase a hundred, and a hundred of you will chase ten thousand, and your enemies will fall before you by the sword. (Leviticus 26:7–8)

These verses show us that there is strength in numbers. Five of God's soldiers can cause one hundred enemy soldiers to fall, but one hundred of God's soldiers can cause ten thousand of the enemy to fall. There is strength in numbers. Yet one dweller knowledgeable in the use of spiritual warfare can effectively cause ten thousand spiritual enemies to fall.

A thousand may fall at your side,
And ten thousand at your right hand;

David was credited with having accomplished that feat and had even felled a nine-foot giant named Goliath with a slingshot and a single smooth stone he had acquired from a nearby brook. If the ten thousand at your right hand mentioned in this verse indicates that we are to be fighting against a host of physical enemies, we as God's people are in trouble. Only the physically strong would be able to come against such a horde. However, just as David was enabled to conquer his physical enemies, so we have been empowered to conquer our spiritual enemies through the Lord Jesus Christ.

The Gospel of Luke tells of an action taken by Jesus on behalf of His followers and informs us about the results that came about because of that action.

> And He called the twelve together, and gave them power and authority over all the demons. (Luke 9:1)

> And the seventy returned with joy, saying, "Lord, even the demons are subject to us in Your name." (Luke 10:17)

Believers have been given power and authority (jurisdiction) over demonic forces with the intention that they use it effectively. Demons are fully aware of that fact. It is the majority of believers that are in the dark on the subject.

Psalm 91:7 tells us that ten thousand fall at the dweller's right hand. Concerning the right hand, Exodus 15 says,

> "Your right hand, O LORD, is majestic in power,
> Your right hand, O LORD, shatters the enemy."
> (Exodus 15:6)

Right-handed people hold their weapon in their right hand, which is stronger and symbolizes power. Ten thousand spiritual enemies fall from a dweller's single-handed spiritual warfare.

A thousand may fall at your side, And ten thousand at your right hand; *But it shall not approach you.*

The word *approach* means to draw close to or to come near. Verse 7 says, "It shall not approach you." To what does the pronoun *it* refer? Does *it* refer to the terror, the arrow, the pestilence, or destruction listed in verses 5 and 6 that comes from the enemy? No, it cannot mean that because those verses tell us that the dweller will not be afraid of those things. They do not tell us they will not come to the dweller. Those who dwell in the shelter of the Most High will not fear them. Certainly, a believer can experience terror, arrows, pestilence, and destruction from the enemy. However uncomfortable the thought, believers are not immune from being attacked by their spiritual enemies.

We must find another explanation for what the word *it* references. Otherwise, verses 5 and 6 contradict verse 7. The word *it* refers to the dweller being defeated by the enemy. The enemy will not defeat the dweller because the enemy cannot find the one who dwells in the secret place/shelter of the Most High. In that position, you can be tempted but need not fall for the enemy's bait. Thus, as a dweller you will not fall in defeat at the hand of the enemy.

An angler throws his lure into the water and hopes a fish will bite, but the fish must still react. The more attractive the bait, the greater the probability of a strike. In like manner, dwellers can be attracted to the enemy's bait. The more attractive and alluring the bait, the greater the probability they can be drawn out of the shelter of the Most High.

As dwellers abide in the shadow of the Almighty, they will not be defeated in spiritual warfare against demonic forces, even though they may bring terror, arrows, pestilence, or destruction our way. Instead dwellers will find themselves basking in the reality of verse 8.

Summary

A thousand may fall at your side, And ten thousand at your right hand; But it shall not approach you.

Although greatly outnumbered, Psalm 91 dwellers will have pursued their enemies and crushed their oppressive attacks. Although many fellow believers may have fallen at the hand of the enemy, dwellers will still be standing when the smoke of battle clears. While the enemy may attempt to overcome Christians, those who dwell in the shelter of the Most High and abide in the shadow of the Almighty will not know defeat at the hand of the enemy.

Psalm 91:8

The Reward of the Wicked

You will only look on with your eyes,
And see the recompense of the wicked.

Because there are no wicked in heaven to observe, those who dwell in the shelter of the Most High are able to see the recompense of the wicked while living on planet Earth. As dwellers find themselves involved in effective spiritual warfare, they will be privileged to see the workers from the kingdom of darkness experience major defeat for their reward. Every time we as dwellers are victorious in spiritual warfare, the enemy takes another mouthful of dust.[110]

We must never forget that demons have the ability and the desire to influence the minds and emotions of people—whether Christian or not. By utilizing that approach, demons intend to give expression to their own vile intentions. By doing so in such a clandestine manner, demons are able to negatively influence their human hosts who, in turn, may vent their emotions on the innocent. Of course, those who are not oppressed can do the same thing on their own apart from any influence from any evil from the supernatural realm. Their flesh is quite adept at such behavior.

The spiritual battles encountered or witnessed by dwellers have been fierce. They have witnessed a thousand comrades fall at their sides simply because of a lack of understanding concerning the workings of the world, the flesh, or the realities of spiritual warfare. Their comrades' fleshly eyes are often fixed upon their circumstances, and they do not comprehend that their demonic enemies have swallowed them up. Their best intentions have proven to be unsuccessful in finding lasting release from their fleshly, worldly, or spiritual bondages.

Yet dwellers have battled not only the flesh and various worldly elements but also demonic forces in the strength of the Lord and prevailed. The rigors of war have strengthened the dwellers' spiritual capacity to discern when the enemy is at work against them. The dwellers' spiritual enemy has personally observed—perhaps for the very first time—the truth that believers do indeed have authority over the forces of darkness.

The Lord has rewarded the dweller's resolve to overcome the blows of his or her enemies. Demonic entities have been humiliated and defeated at the hand of a being that is totally dependent upon the Lord for victory.

No amount of spiritual battle has deterred dwellers from implementing biblically sound spiritual warfare tactics against their enemies. God is pleased, and the enemy suffers a major defeat. As a dweller, you will observe this with your spiritual eyes and will see the wicked receive their just reward. First Corinthians 6 echoes agreement.

> Do you not know that we will judge angels? (1 Corinthians 6:3)

Psalm 103 says,

> Bless the LORD, you His angels, Mighty in strength, who perform His word, Obeying the voice of His word! (Psalm 103:20)

Obviously, this judging of angels is not referring to God's holy angels. There is no judgment needed for them since they are faithful in carrying out the commands and wishes of God. The judgment spoken of in 1 Corinthians 6:3 is referring to fallen angels that followed and fell with Lucifer once he declared that he would be like the Most High.[111]

Ephesians 6 sets the parameters for the spiritual battle in which believers must wage war.

> For our struggle is not against flesh and blood, but against the rulers, against the powers, against the world forces of this darkness, against the spiritual forces of wickedness in the heavenly places. (Ephesians 6:12)

This verse informs us that our spiritual battles will be fought against four levels of demonic entities, specifically

1. rulers,
2. powers,
3. world forces of this darkness, and
4. spiritual forces of wickedness in the heavenly places.

Let's take a brief look at Paul's hierarchy of demonic forces that believers struggle against.

Rulers

The word for *rulers* in the Greek language is *arche*, which refers to "the person or thing that commences, the first person or thing in a series, the leader."[112] A ruler has received his commission and his orders.

This refers to the first demon to gain authority to operate within an individual. A ruler demon assigned to a person or a family is a first in a series. The ruler is the leader. A ruler demon living inside a person is the strong man that must be cast out and is the first demon to enter into that person. The strong man is not necessarily the strongest demon, but he is the first demon to enter a person. The ruler has authority over the other demons that indwell the person. When Jesus dealt with Legion and those under his authority in the Gadarene demoniac, He was dealing with a ruler demon.[113]

Powers

The word for *powers* in the Greek language is *exousia*.

> *Exousia,* as a noun denotes "authority" (from the impersonal verb *exesti* "it is lawful").[114]

In Ephesians 6:12, this second group of angelic beings is called "powers." Thayer defines *powers* as follows:

> The power of rule or government (the power of him whose will and commands must be submitted to by others and obeyed) … [and have the] authority to manage domestic affairs … The leading and more powerful among created beings superior to man, spiritual potentates.[115]

Romans 13:1 says,

> Let every person be in subjection to the governing authorities. For there is no authority except from God, and those which exist are established by God. (Romans 13:1)

The designation of powers refers to a higher-level demon that would have the God-given right to exercise authority over their assigned city, county, or state.

World Forces of this Darkness

The Greek word *Kosmokrator* is translated as "world forces of this darkness." This cannot be referring to Satan since it is used in the plural.

> *Kosmokrator* … signifies a "ruler" of the whole world, a world-lord … The context ("not against flesh and blood") shows that not earthly potentates are indicated, but spirit powers, who, under the permissive will of God, and in consequence of human sin, exercise Satanic and therefore antagonistic authority over the world in its present condition of spiritual darkness and alienation from God.[116]

Some would classify a *Kosmokrator* as a "territorial" demon. A demon of this rank would have a great deal of power. The NASB refers to this demon as "world forces of this darkness." Darkness can refer to darkened eyesight or blindness. This category of demon would attempt to blind the spiritual eyes of those under its jurisdiction.

A *Kosmokrator* refers to demons assigned over nations. Daniel 10 provides an example. For three weeks, Daniel had humbled himself before God. As Daniel had a vision, a messenger angel spoke to him.

> Then he said to me, "Do not be afraid, Daniel, for from the first day that you set your heart on understanding this and on humbling yourself before your God, your words were heard, and I have come in response to your words. But the prince of the kingdom of Persia was withstanding me for twenty-one days; then behold, Michael, one of the chief princes, came to help me, for I had been left there with the kings of Persia." (Daniel 10:12–13)

The prince of the kingdom of Persia delayed an angel that God had sent with a message for Daniel.

> Daniel's prayer was heard on the first day of the three week period, but the answer was delayed because of angelic warfare.[117]

According to the angel that God had sent to give a message to Daniel, this angelic warfare was initiated and fought by a *Kosmokrator*, a powerful spirit identified as the prince of the kingdom of Persia.

Spiritual Forces of Wickedness

These spiritual forces of wickedness are described by the Greek word *poneria*. The word is defined by Thayer as "depravity, iniquity, wickedness, malice: evil purposes and desires."[118]

This would refer to the demonic forces that oppress believers from without. Paul, James, and Peter warned us about these demons. It is our responsibility to battle this group of demons as they attempt to oppress us. James said it like this:

> Submit therefore to God. Resist the devil and he will flee from you. (James 4:7)

We must first submit to God. If we are not under proper submission to God in our life, a demon is under no obligation to obey us. Once we submit, it is then our responsibility and privilege to resist any demon that is oppressing us. Once we use scripturally sound principles, the demon will flee from us.

Summary

**You will only look on with your eyes,
And see the recompense of the wicked.**

Dwellers have witnessed fellow believers become battle casualties in the spiritual conflict with the enemy because of either their uninformed stance on warfare or their failure to implement sound spiritual warfare principles. Dwellers, however, have not been lackadaisical in their dealings with their spiritual enemies. In their various battles, they may encounter rulers, powers, world forces of this darkness, and other spiritual forces of wickedness in heavenly places. They have recognized, encountered, and successfully defeated them in the strength of the Lord, who has promised that dwellers will observe their antagonists getting their just reward.

Notes

Psalm 91:9

The Commitment

For you have made the LORD, my refuge,
Even the Most High, your dwelling place.

"For you have made." How did you do that? How has this been accomplished in your life? An example may prove helpful.

At some point in your life, you decide you want to attend college and earn a degree. After carefully considering your interests, desires, and plans, you investigate a number of institutions of higher learning that interest you and then you make your final choice. You send in your application, are accepted, and finally begin your classes. You are now a college student. Your actions in and out of class demonstrate that you are a serious student with a goal. Yet many of your classmates are not as enthusiastic about their studies. At times they may even encourage you to relax and have some well-deserved fun, but you remain steadfast. You have decided to earn a degree and let nothing get in your way. As expected, your upper-division classes require extra time, effort, and perseverance, but they bring you closer to your goal. The day of graduation finally arrives, and you receive your long-awaited degree! Because of your graduation, you are no longer a college student. *You have made* the transition. Note that it was your decision to enter into college and earn a degree. However, the choice of curriculum was not under your control. Your alma mater made that determination and even set the standard required for earning the degree. Once you achieved that standard, it was ascertained that you had been successful in your field of study, and your coveted degree was awarded.

"For you have made." Verse 2 is no longer pie in the sky. It is reality. At some point in your Christian walk, you made the choice to follow God fully. Your surrender and commitment to Him were genuine and heartfelt. You may have undergone life experiences that were out of your control, and they were tough to understand and navigate. You certainly would not have chosen the curriculum. Another predetermined it. At times, your logic and reason have been at odds concerning what God has required of you, but you have followed His leading. Some of your Christian friends may have thought you were a bit too serious about your Christianity. Nonetheless, you have persevered.

In life's experiences, you have learned to turn to Jehovah as your refuge and fortress. Worry is no longer a part of your vocabulary. You have come to understand what it means to trust God and have grown past the lip service of the past. Trusting God is no longer an issue because "you have made." When we actually come to comprehend and comply with Psalm 91:2, we are dwellers. We cannot go back because we have made a vow to God, and He will require it of us. Dwellers are saying that regardless of the bad or evil circumstances that find them, Jehovah is their refuge and fortress. They have put their trust in their God.

Dwellers no longer take refuge in their flesh. Nor are they being overcome by it. Rather they have mentally experienced serving the law of God.[119] They do not live "after the flesh." They are more practiced at crucifying the inappropriate deeds of the body. Dwellers understand that the name of the LORD is a strong tower. Emotions certainly do play a part, but they do not dictate the dweller's course of action.

"You have made ..." You have taken on some of the characteristics of the LORD and are becoming more like the Most High. As Satan and the kingdom of darkness observe your victories as a dweller, they must be reminded of the words spoken by their Creator and Judge.

> "And dust shall you eat all the days of your life."
> (Genesis 3:14)

"You have made," even though the enemy has done his best to cause fear. He has lied to you, brought his own form of pestilence, and engaged you in fierce spiritual warfare.

In verse 1, we found it was necessary for the would-be dweller to make the choice to dwell. As we make that choice, God's part is to prune us, so to speak, so that His attributes begin to take root and grow in our own soul. For example, Galatians 5 tells us about the fruit of the Spirit.

> But the fruit of the Spirit is love, joy, peace, patience, kindness, goodness, faithfulness, gentleness, self-control; against such things there is no law.
> (Galatians 5:22–23)

As believers, we oftentimes read the words accurately but do not apprehend their meaning. In these verses, we are told that the fruit of the Spirit *is*. Then a list follows—love, joy, peace, patience, kindness, goodness, faithfulness, gentleness, and self-control. The way these verses play out in our lives may actually be quite different. We may live as though it reads like this: The fruit of the Spirit *could be, should be, or will be some day*. In other words, when I get my act together, I will experience the fruit of the Spirit. However, that is *not* what Scripture says. Scripture declares that the fruit of the Spirit *is*.

When a person is born again, the Spirit of God and the spirit of that individual are joined together.[120] When the Holy Spirit enters into our spirit, do we suppose He leaves His fruit behind? No, He brings it with Him. Therefore, *all* the fruit of the Spirit is encased within our human spirit. We cannot do anything to get more of the Spirit's fruit because it is already there—just as the Holy Spirit is there.

What resides in each Christian's spirit needs to take root in the soul. That is the process of sanctification.

> Sanctification means the progressive conforming of the believer into the image of Christ, or the process by which the life is made morally holy.[121]

Our flesh, of course, objects to such things, and Paul tells us why that is so.

> But I say, walk by the Spirit, and you will not carry out the desire of the flesh. For the flesh sets its desire against the Spirit, and the Spirit against the flesh; for these are in opposition to one another, so that you may not do the things that you please. (Galatians 5:16–17)

Our inner man joyfully concurs with the law of God.[122] Our flesh, on the other hand, is not as gleeful and may act more like a spoiled, self-centered two-year-old who wants what he wants when he wants it. In some, the flesh is more determined to oppose the desires of the Spirit—much like a strong-willed child might resist unwanted instruction from an authority figure. When the flesh is in control and the will concedes to the desires of the flesh, the inner man is outvoted and will thus be kept in the background. For change to occur, it is necessary for the will to choose to yield to the desires of the Spirit. The more aggressively the flesh fights against the Spirit, the longer it takes for the process of sanctification to occur.

Verse 1 has given us the facts. If we dwell in the shelter of the Most High, we will abide in the shadow of the Almighty. By the time you experientially arrive at verse 9, the foregoing facts have become a reality in your experience, "for you have made." A positive transition has taken place. You left one place and have gone to another. You are now in a different place. The Most High is now your dwelling place.

Notice that the words "For you have made" are written in the past tense. The Hebrew language expresses a completed action. You have made the choice to take refuge in the LORD and to dwell from your spirit under the protective umbrella of the Most High.

Dwellers are made, not born. When we become Christians, we do not automatically become dwellers. At some point in our Christian lives, we may come to the place where we make the choice to dwell. Making that choice, however, does not immediately transform us into dwellers any more than entering college would result in procuring an immediate degree. Nevertheless, that choice does catapult us into a new learning curve that is designed to deepen our understanding and trust of God. Dwelling, therefore, occurs not only because of a choice we make but also because of what we must learn. We must meet specific requirements before we can consistently dwell. So the questions before us are as follows: "How does a believer become a dweller? What must take place or what must we learn before the transformation to a dweller can occur?"

Let us briefly review the qualifications involved in becoming a dweller and being able to trust the LORD to be your refuge and fortress. They are found in Psalm 91:3–8.

The Making of a Dweller

Psalm 91:3

For it is He who delivers you from the snare of the trapper, And from the deadly pestilence.

We must first learn and understand that we are responsible for fighting our spiritual enemies and that we cannot defeat these enemies in our own strength or through our own resources. As we learn to overcome and crucify the deeds of the flesh, submit to the leadership of the Holy Spirit within, and utilize the truth given in the Word, God delivers us from the snare of the trapper. That does not mean we can never be snared. David was snared when he chose to rely upon the numbers of his warriors and chariots instead of relying upon God.[123] Satan attempted to ensnare Jesus in the wilderness.[124] However, He was a living example of Psalm 91:9. Since He was abiding in the Father, the tempter had no choice but to flee when Jesus told him to go.

Although 1 Timothy 3:7 warns about being snared by the devil, dwellers have the assurance that the LORD will deliver them from the *snare* of the trapper. Because of our determined obedience to the commands and requirements of the LORD, He delivers us from the deadly pestilence.

Psalm 91:4

He will cover you with His pinions And under His wings you may seek refuge; His faithfulness is a shield and bulwark.

We learn to run to the Lord in times of trouble instead of depending upon our own ingenuity, our finances, our flesh, or any other ways we may have of coping. We learn that God's faithfulness (truth) is our shield that will protect us from lies and wrong thinking. Jesus used the truth of the Word as a sword against the devil when He said, "It is written." As He quoted Scripture, He used the shield of faith to extinguish the flaming missiles of the evil one.[125] We must learn to seek refuge under the umbrella of God's protective care and to utilize His truth as our shield and bulwark.

Psalm 91:5

You will not be afraid of the terror by night, Or of the arrow that flies by day.

Although our spiritual enemies relish the opportunity to bring fear to the people of God, dwellers have learned to exercise authority over oppressing demons without fear. They have also learned to recognize the arrows the enemy launches by way of contaminated thoughts and feelings. Dwellers realize the importance of taking every thought captive to the obedience of Christ.[126]

Psalm 91:6

Of the pestilence that stalks in darkness, Or of the destruction that lays waste at noon.

Dwellers have a deeper understanding of the importance of Scripture in warding off the enemy's stalking. They are no longer in the dark concerning the issue of spiritual warfare and are alert to the pestilence that their spiritual enemies can bring. Although dwellers have faced some of the enemies' tactics used in warfare, they do not fear their adversaries' destructive capabilities.

Psalm 91:7

A thousand may fall at your side And ten thousand at your right hand, But it shall not approach you.

Although dwellers may witness fellow Christians falling to the tactics of the world, the flesh, and the devil, they will have learned to effectively fight their flesh, overcome the allure of the world, and engage in combative spiritual warfare against their spiritual enemies. As an abiding dweller, you will experience demons falling by your hand and know that they can do nothing about it—although they may boast, challenge, and attempt to defeat you in the process. The dweller is no longer falling in battle under the oppressive hand of the enemy.

Psalm 91:8

You will only look on with your eyes, And see the recompense of the wicked.

The wicked include the rulers, the powers, the world forces of this darkness, and the spiritual forces of wickedness in heavenly places. Dwellers have the responsibility to be on the alert for the activity of demons in their own lives and in the lives of other believers.[127] When you as a dweller exercise the spiritual authority God has given you over the kingdom of darkness,[128] you will see the enemy reap their just reward.[129]

For you have made *the LORD,*

In the book of Genesis, the LORD told Adam what he was to do and informed him of the consequences should he choose to disobey.

> And the LORD God commanded the man, saying, "From any tree of the garden you may eat freely; but from the tree of the knowledge of good and evil you shall not eat, for in the day that you eat from it you shall surely die." (Genesis 2:16–17)

Sometime later when the serpent came on the scene and offered Adam and Eve an opportunity to either believe the LORD or to believe the tempter's lie, the newly formed couple chose to believe the lie. How did the LORD respond? He first brought judgment upon the serpent and then upon the woman and then upon Adam.

When Psalm 91:9 says, "For you have made the LORD, even the Most High your dwelling place," it means we have come to understand that we must be obedient to His commands. This is further emphasized when we are told to be holy because the LORD our God is holy.[130] As the LORD's people, we are to be set apart and devoted to Him for His use. In order to make the LORD our dwelling place, we must live holy lives.

For you have made the LORD, *my refuge,*

Dwellers have declared that the LORD is their refuge. A refuge is a shelter or a place of protection from danger. It is a safe place and could be compared to a refuge where different species of wildlife are protected. The LORD is a place of safety. He is our refuge.[131]

Because of what goes on from verses 2 through 8, dwellers have developed a friendship bond with the LORD. As they dwell, they go to His secret place to be with the LORD Most High, who is their dwelling place. Dwellers run to Him because they love Him.[132] When we dwell, we are not simply running to a place but to a Person.

To make the Lord your dwelling place requires more than just a choice or simply acquiring more head knowledge. By the time you come to personally experience the reality of Psalm 91:9, you have come to a clearer spiritual realization of what the nature of the Lord really is. You have a better spiritual understanding and enlightenment concerning the Lord, and in your daily life, you have begun to incorporate His values as your own.

Experiencing the fruit of the Spirit in your everyday life is not just a dream. As a dweller, the fruit of the Spirit is being expressed in the soul. For example, I once spoke to a man known for his verbal abuse. Fearing the worst, I silently reiterated my choice to dwell in the shelter of the Most High before our meeting. True to his nature, the man utilized his abusive tactics in an attempt to intimidate. Normally, my flesh would have become quite defensive and cleverly tried to overcome his rejecting, abusive comments. My emotions would have displayed a nonspiritual attitude by throwing up invisible walls as a defense mechanism. Instead an amazing thing took place. During his ranting and raving, my mind remained calm and understanding. I felt compassion for him, even though his verbalizations and conclusions were inaccurate. My will chose to forgive even though the wrong he had committed had not been made right. I did not have the ability to bring conscientiousness or change to the man, but at that moment I did have the ability, the right, and the responsibility to allow Christ to live His life through me and to be my refuge in a troubling time.

> **For you have made the LORD, my refuge,**
> *Even the Most High, your dwelling place.*

Psalm 91:9 takes the meaning of verse 1 to a more personal level. Whereas verse 1 is a general statement, verse 9 reveals that a commitment has been made. It is interesting to note that Psalm 7 uses the term LORD Most High.

> I will give thanks to the LORD according to His righteousness And will sing praise to the name of the LORD Most High. (Psalm 7:17)

We could read Psalm 91:9 as follows and not do injustice to the verse or change its meaning: "For you have made the LORD Most High your dwelling place."

The LORD Most High is your dwelling place, not your spirit. When we dwell, we are not putting faith in our spirit. We are putting our faith in the LORD Most High, who lives in our spirit. As you choose to operate from your spirit, you are in His refuge. You cannot be functioning from the natural resources available to your soul and expect to simultaneously dwell in the refuge of the Most High. When you dwell, you are not simply running to your spirit. You are running to the LORD Most High, who is united with your spirit. The LORD Most High is the dweller's shelter/secret place. Psalm 32 gives this declaration:

You are my hiding place; You preserve me from trouble; You surround me with songs of deliverance. Selah. (Psalm 32:7)

The term for hiding place used in Psalm 32:7 is the same Hebrew word used in Psalm 91:1. "He who dwells in the shelter (secret place) of the Most High." When we have made the LORD Most High our dwelling place, He will enable us to discover whom our spiritual enemies are, so we can utilize what He has taught us. Then we will defeat them, because He will deliver our enemies into our hands.

This was illustrated when Abram was living by the Oaks of Mamre. The kings of the region had been at war and had captured Abram's nephew, Lot, along with his possessions. That did not set well with Abram, so he led his own little army in pursuit, defeated his enemies, and recovered what the enemy had taken, including Lot. Then he met up with Melchizedek, king of Salem,[133] who told Abram that it was the Most High who had delivered Abram's enemies into his hand. The Most High will do the same thing for the dweller.

The LORD Most High is your dwelling place. He is united with your spirit, and He blesses the dwelling of the righteous.[134] This is the reason you can take a fearless stance concerning the enemy. "You have made" is not just a one-time choice. Becoming a dweller is a process that leads to a lifestyle. Through various temptations and tests, you have been faithful to see the LORD as your refuge and the Most High as your dwelling place.

Summary

For you have made the Lord, my refuge,
Even the Most High, your dwelling place.

At this point in the psalm, a major change has taken place in the life of the one who has painstakingly traversed through the first eight verses of Psalm 91. The one who has experienced the journey is no longer a spectator simply observing those who dwell. He or she is an active participant. The first eight verses of Psalm 91 have given the qualifications for becoming a dweller. If you have made the Lord Most High your refuge and your dwelling place, the Lord has been grooming you and is in the process of preparing you for additional service.

Psalm 91:10

No Evil Will Befall You

No evil will befall you,
Nor will any plague come near your tent.

The enemy may use this verse to try to deliver guilt and condemnation to those who do not understand it. For example, if you find yourself in the middle of some tragic situation, the enemy could easily say, "Has not the Lord said that no evil will befall you? Is the situation in which you find yourself not evil? Does this very situation not prove to you that God's Word is not as true for you as you would like to believe? Now let me tell you the truth of the matter."[135]

Evil Defined and Illustrated

The Hebrew word for *evil* in this verse is defined as "distress, misery, injury, and calamity."[136] This form of evil can influence a person whether it comes by way of evil words, evil thoughts, or evil actions that are perpetrated against us. Strong's adds this explanation of *evil*:

This word combines together in one the wicked deed and its consequences. It generally indicates the rough exterior of wrongdoing as a breach of harmony and as breaking up of what is good and desirable in man and in society. While the prominent characteristic of the godly is lovingkindness (2617), one of the most marked features of the ungodly man is that his course is an injury both to himself and to everyone around him.[137]

According to Pastor Brewster Porcella, a contributor in the Zondervan Pictorial Bible Dictionary, *evil* is

[a] term designating that which is not in harmony with the divine order ... Moral evil, or sin, is any lack of conformity to the moral law of God. According to the Bible, it is the cause of the existence of physical or natural evil in this world.[138]

• In the Life of Joseph

Joseph would be an example from a human perspective of how evil could attempt to influence a child of God. When Joseph was seventeen,[139] he had two dreams that he related to his brothers and to his parents. In essence, the dreams foretold that his family would someday bow down and pay homage to Joseph. The dreams gave the already jealous brothers even more reason to hate their youngest brother.

One day Joseph's father sent his favorite son to check on his brothers and on the flocks. When the brothers saw the dreamer coming, they schemed against him and planned to put him to death. Jacob's oldest son, Rueben, opposed that scheme, and the brothers wound up selling Joseph to some passing Ishmaelites. They, in turn, sold him in Egypt to Pharaoh's officer Potiphar, the captain of the bodyguard.

To cover their tracks, the brothers killed a goat, dipped Joseph's multicolored tunic in the goat blood, and presented the garment to their father. As he beheld the evidence his sons provided, Jacob fell into deep mourning because of the fate that he believed had befallen his beloved son.

Meanwhile, as Joseph found himself in the service of Potiphar, the officer's wife falsely accused Joseph of sexual misconduct. As a result, Joseph was thrown into jail. Psalm 105 offers some specifics concerning this particular time in the life of Joseph.

> He sent a man before them, Joseph, who was sold as a slave. They afflicted his feet with fetters, He himself was laid in irons; Until the time that his word came to pass, The word of the LORD tested him. (Psalm 105:17–19)

Even during his incarceration, the LORD's favor was upon Jacob's son. While imprisoned, Pharaoh's chief cupbearer and his chief baker were also thrown into jail. In due time, both had dreams that Joseph accurately interpreted. Years later Pharaoh had an unsettling dream that his royal staff members were unable to interpret, so he sent for the young, imprisoned Hebrew and related his dream. God gave Joseph the interpretation, which involved an upcoming, severe famine in the land. Joseph also provided instructions as to what should be done because of the approaching calamity. Because of Joseph's God-given interpretation, Pharaoh was pleased, and Joseph was elevated to second-in-command over the land of Egypt.

Joseph put God's instruction into motion and saved grain from the bountiful harvests for seven years. True to the interpretation of the dream, the resulting famine was right on schedule and was so widespread that it also affected Joseph's family in the land of Canaan. After Joseph's father heard that there was grain available in Egypt, he sent his sons to purchase some much-needed provisions.

When the brothers went before Joseph, they did not recognize him. Regardless, Joseph recognized them. When Joseph questioned the brothers, they told him who they were and why they were in Egypt, and they also informed Joseph that their youngest brother, Benjamin, had remained in Canaan with their father. Joseph accused them of being spies and told them he would test what they were saying by requiring them to bring their youngest brother to him. He then imprisoned one brother named Simeon and let the others return to Canaan with their supplies.

The brothers knew that what they had done to Joseph as a teenager was wrong. Genesis 42 captured their sentiment.

> Then they said to one another, "Truly we are guilty concerning our brother, because we saw the distress of his soul when he pleaded with us, yet we would not listen; therefore this distress has come upon us."
> (Genesis 42:21)

With heavy hearts, the brothers returned home and related the events of their journey into Egypt to their father. Time passed, and once again, their food supply dwindled. For a second time, the brothers were sent back to Egypt for more grain. On this second visit, as required, they brought their youngest brother, Benjamin, with them. Joseph had them eat a meal at his home before they were all sent back to Canaan with their provisions. Unbeknownst to the brothers, Joseph had his house steward place Joseph's silver cup into Benjamin's grain sack. Soon after the brothers left for home, Joseph instructed his house steward to go after them, accuse them of stealing his silver cup, and bring them back. Upon their return, they reviewed why they had come in the first place and why Benjamin needed to return to his father.

Joseph, however, could control his emotions no longer. He made himself known to his brothers and reassured them. His words are found in Genesis 45.

"And now do not be grieved or angry with yourselves, because you sold me here; for God sent me before you to preserve life. For the famine has been in the land these two years, and there are still five years in which there will be neither plowing nor harvesting. And God sent me before you to preserve for you a remnant in the earth, and to keep you alive by a great deliverance. Now, therefore, it was not you who sent me here, but God; and He has made me a father to Pharaoh and lord of all his household and ruler over all the land of Egypt." (Genesis 45:5–8)

Joseph realized that although his brothers had sold him into slavery and that he had reaped the unfavorable consequences of their actions, God was very much in the picture. God was, in fact, making provision for Joseph's family far in advance of their actual physical needs that would soon arise.

When Pharaoh heard that Joseph's brothers were in the land of Egypt, he provided them with all they would need to move Joseph's family to Egypt. He even promised to give them the best of Egypt's land in which to live. Therefore, Joseph's brothers returned to their father in the land of Canaan and told him the good news concerning Joseph. Jacob's response is enlightening and reveals a truth that is largely unheard yet rings true to this very day.

Then they went up from Egypt, and came to the land of Canaan to their father Jacob. They told him, saying, "Joseph is still alive, and indeed he is ruler over all the land of Egypt." But he was stunned, for he did not believe them. When they told him all the words of Joseph that he had spoken to them, and when he saw the wagons that Joseph had sent to carry him, the spirit of their father Jacob revived. Then Israel said, "It is enough; my son Joseph is still

alive. I will go and see him before I die." (Genesis
45:25–28)

When Joseph was promoted to second-in-command to
Pharaoh, he was thirty years of age. When his brothers came for
grain from the land of Canaan, Joseph was thirty-nine.[140] When
Joseph's brothers returned to Jacob with the provisions that Joseph
had sent to enable their move to Egypt, the spirit of Jacob revived.
That means that Jacob had mourned for Joseph for more than
twenty years. Had Jacob been in mourning because a wild beast
had killed Joseph at the age of seventeen? A wild beast had not
killed Joseph. Joseph was alive and well, yet Jacob remained in
mourning for more than twenty years because he had listened
to—and believed—a lie!

When Jacob saw the wagons that Joseph had sent, his *spirit*
revived. Jacob's spirit had been affected for more than twenty
years because he had believed a lie. From the information given
in Psalm 91:10, it would be safe to conclude that Jacob was not
dwelling in the shelter of the Most High during those twenty
years. Rather he was operating from his soul. Thus, his spirit
continued to be overwhelmed until he heard and accepted the
truth. How many Christians are there today whose spirit is in need
of being revived because they have unintentionally believed some
lie that they have accepted as truth?

Jacob moved to Egypt and enjoyed the produce of that land
for seventeen years. At the age of 147, Jacob died.[141] Soon after,
Joseph's brothers became fearful that Joseph might bear a grudge
against them and repay them for the wrong they had committed
against him, so they sent him the following message:

> "Your father charged before he died, saying, 'Thus
> you shall say to Joseph, "Please forgive, I beg you,
> the transgression of your brothers and their sin, for
> they did you wrong."' And now, please forgive the
> transgression of the servants of the God of your

father." And Joseph wept when they spoke to him. (Genesis 50:16–17)

Then Joseph answered his brothers' concerns and said,

> "And as for you, you meant evil against me, but God meant it for good in order to bring about this present result, to preserve many people alive. So therefore, do not be afraid; I will provide for you and your little ones." So he comforted them and spoke kindly to them. (Genesis 50:20–21)

Joseph called their actions evil, but he understood that God had allowed it for a divine purpose. Nowhere in Scripture do we have any hint that Joseph's spirit was affected by his varied circumstances. Rather he trusted in the LORD and was blessed. Scripture provides ample evidence that Joseph's experience is a testimony to the value of dwelling in the shelter of the Most High.

No evil will befall you ...

Psalm 91:10 refers to the dweller, not the nondweller. The context of the present psalm does not allow evil to befall the dweller. If this phrase was also referring to a nondweller being exempt from any evil, the verse would be moot and would serve no purpose. There would be no benefit from dwelling since no evil would befall either group. Evil, though, can definitely influence the nondweller.

Neither can the phrase under consideration be referring to nothing bad ever happening to a dweller or to a nondweller because from a human perspective, evil things definitely happen to both groups. The issue at hand necessitates having a proper point of view.

The word *befall* means to "encounter or to approach."[142] Before we can find out what this means, we need to find out what it does *not* mean. The phrase "no evil will befall you" does not mean that no evil people or circumstances will ever come your way.

Until the Lord returns, evil will always be around. The testimony of Scripture clearly demonstrates that evil circumstances will certainly cross the Christian's path. Therefore, the phrase "no evil will befall you" cannot mean that no evil circumstances will ever come our way as Christians. The following words of Jesus in the Gospel of John shed light on the subject.

> "This is the judgment, that the Light has come into the world, and men loved the darkness rather than the Light, for their deeds were evil." (John 3:19)

Jesus said that men in darkness would engage in evil deeds. Paul gives this admonition concerning evil:

> Do not be overcome by evil, but overcome evil with good. (Romans 12:21)

If we say Psalm 91:10 means no evil thing or circumstance will befall you, then what about David who had been anointed king yet was pursued by King Saul, who intended to kill him?[143] What about John the Baptist who was beheaded?[144] What about Paul, who was imprisoned, beaten with rods, shipwrecked, in danger of death, five times received thirty-nine lashes, and was stoned? What about Jesus who was crucified?[145]

"No evil will befall you" cannot mean that as you are dwelling, no evil circumstances will come your way. Jesus was a dweller, yet He was crucified. Does His crucifixion not prove He was dwelling? Had He not been dwelling, would He have allowed His crucifixion to occur? He easily could have called upon legions of angels to provide an immediate rescue.[146] Now look at the documentation given in Hebrews 11.

> Women received *back* their dead by resurrection; and others were tortured, not accepting their release, in order that they might obtain a better resurrection; and others experienced mockings and scourgings, yes, also chains and imprisonment. They were stoned, they were sawn in two, they were

tempted, they were put to death with the sword; they went about in sheepskins, in goatskins, being destitute, afflicted, ill-treated (men of whom the world was not worthy), wandering in deserts and mountains and caves and holes in the ground. (Hebrews 11:35–38)

From a human perspective, the phrase "No evil will befall you" cannot mean that no evil circumstance will come upon you as a Christian, even as a dweller. From most people's perspective, being sawed in two would certainly be considered evil! It is possible for evil to negatively touch a dwelling believer physically, emotionally, financially, socially, psychologically, and materially but not spiritually. Evil unquestionably befell Paul physically, yet in spirit he held fast to his convictions and was not adversely affected.

- **When Is Evil Not Evil?**

On the other hand, Romans 8 provides some insightful words.

> And we know that God causes all things to work together for good to those who love God, to those who are called according to His purpose. (Romans 8:28)

From a human perspective, evil circumstances do occur in a Christian's life. Even when they do, God will cause those things to work together for our good. From God's perspective, however, whatever is allowed in our life that is intended to conform us increasingly into the image of Jesus Christ is not considered as evil. That is why after being sold into slavery, being falsely accused, and being thrown into jail that Joseph could say to his brothers,

> "As for you, you meant evil against me, but God meant it for good in order to bring about this present

result, to preserve many people alive." (Genesis 50:20–21)

Listen to the admonition found in the book of Proverbs.

The fear of the LORD is the beginning of knowledge; fools despise wisdom and instruction. (Proverbs 1:7)

"But he who listens to me shall live securely, And will be at ease from the dread of evil." (Proverbs 1:33)

The word *live* in verse 33 carries with it the idea of lodging, to reside or permanently stay, to dwell.[147] The KJV says it like this:

But whoso hearkeneth unto me shall dwell safely, and shall be quiet from fear of evil. (Proverbs 1:33 KJV)

We can dwell or live securely when we are in a place that offers refuge. John Gill comments on the last phrase of Proverbs 1:33.

And shall be quiet from fear of evil; as they may be in the present life, under a comfortable sense of the blood, righteousness, and sacrifice of Christ: which, when applied and laid hold on by faith, speak peace to the conscience, and yield quietness of mind; so that such have no reason to be afraid of the evil one, Satan, who cannot devour and destroy them; nor of the evil of sin; for, though they may and should be afraid to commit it, yet not of being conquered by it, and coming under the dominion of it, nor of being brought by it into a state of condemnation; nor of the evil of judgments upon a wicked world; nor of death and a future judgment; nor of hell, and everlasting damnation: and hereafter such will enter into peace, and be free from all evils, natural, moral, or spiritual; and from the fear of them, being out of the reach of them all.[148]

- **Evil from Within**

Genesis 6 reveals that evil from within is not a new concept.

> Then the LORD saw that the wickedness of man was great on the earth, and that every intent of the thoughts of his heart was only evil continually. (Genesis 6:5)

Because of the ever-present evil of the unrighteous, God instructed Noah to build an ark and brought a flood upon the earth to purge it. During His time on earth, Jesus spoke to the Pharisees and told them that they were evil and that they spoke from that which filled their hearts.[149] Jesus taught His disciples about the evilness of the heart in Matthew 15.

> "Do you not understand that everything that goes into the mouth passes into the stomach, and is eliminated? But the things that proceed out of the mouth come from the heart, and those defile the man. For out of the heart come evil thoughts, murders, adulteries, fornications, thefts, false witness, slanders. These are the things which defile the man." (Matthew 15:17–20)

In Luke 12, Jesus added this perspective:

> "For where your treasure is, there will your heart be also." (Luke 12:34)

The evil Jesus was speaking about comes from within the heart. The phrase "No evil will befall you" in this psalm is referring to those who dwell in the shelter of the Most High. As the evil in our heart is exposed and comes under the knife of the Master Surgeon, dwellers yield to the Surgeon's purposes and choose to crucify the flesh with its passions and desires.[150] Thus, they become increasingly conformed to the image of Christ each time the process repeats itself.

As a result, the evil in the heart is being replaced with attitudes and responses that more closely represent the character of God. Hebrews 10 offers this assurance:

> Let us draw near with a sincere heart in full assurance of faith, having our hearts sprinkled clean from an evil conscience and our bodies washed with pure water. (Hebrews 10:22)

As dwellers undergo the process of sanctification, the evil in the heart diminishes and loses its deadly grip. Although dwellers can still be tempted and retain the ability to fail, their new nature is in control and more closely mirrors the characteristics of their God. As they are obedient, they can be assured that the evil from within will not befall them.

• **Demonic Evil**

We are given a glimpse of the evilness in the demonic realm as we look at Psalm 78.

> He sent upon them His burning anger, Fury, and indignation, and trouble, A band of destroying angels. (Psalm 78:49)

The KJV says it this way:

> He cast upon them the fierceness of his anger, wrath, and indignation, and trouble, by sending evil angels among them. (Psalm 78:49 KJV)

The NASB uses the term "destroying angels" whereas the KJV uses the term "evil angels." These angels destroyed the firstborn of the Egyptians during the time of Moses's leadership. The word translated as "destroying" and "evil" (used in the NASB and the KJV in Psalm 78:49) is the same word for evil used in Psalm 91:10 that we are considering. The demonic evil referred to in this psalm will not approach the dweller. The dweller's spirit cannot be sabotaged by demonic evil because he or she is dwelling in the shelter of the Most High.

When evil attempts to influence a Christian, the spirit is commonly influenced as well—as we saw in the case of Jacob. Though they are Christians, nondwellers are controlled from their soul or body, and their spirits can be indirectly affected. The book of Job tells how Job's spirit and soul were affected by Satan's attack.

> "Therefore I will not restrain my mouth; I will speak in the anguish of my spirit, I will complain in the bitterness of my soul." (Job 7:11)

> "My spirit is broken, my days are extinguished, The grave is ready for me." (Job 17:1)

There are similarities between the dweller and the fleshly Christian. Both have eternal life and will go to heaven. Both can experience hell on earth, but neither will reside there. There are also dissimilarities between the dweller and the fleshly. First Corinthians 3 reveals some of those differences.

> Now if any man builds on the foundation with gold, silver, precious stones, wood, hay, straw, each man's work will become evident; for the day will show it because it is to be revealed with fire, and the fire itself will test the quality of each man's work. If any man's work which he has built on it remains, he will receive a reward. If any man's work is burned up, he will suffer loss; but he himself shall be saved, yet so as through fire. (1 Corinthians 3:12–15)

The works of those who dwell in the shelter of the Most High are fireproof, whereas the works of the fleshly are combustible. Thus, they lose their reward. The spirit of the fleshly gives in to the demands of the soul and/or body whereas dwellers bring both into subjection.[151]

In the context of Psalm 91, to what does "No evil will befall you" refer? As we have seen, the word *befall* means to encounter or approach. Evil demonic forces will not be able to continually affect you now in the present as a dweller as they have in the past as a fleshly nondweller or as a spiritual nondweller. The reason? Dwellers have learned to recognize demonic oppression, have taken ground back that the enemy had gained, have exercised their authority as believers, and have forced their demonic opponents to leave. Should a fleshly or spiritual believer take authority over an oppressive demon and instruct it to leave, it will keep returning to oppress as long as it retains the legal right to do so.

The context of Psalm 91:10 refers to the one who dwells in the shelter of the Most High. In the wake of a personal calamity, dwellers run to the Most High who lives in their spirit. The real you is your spirit. Your body is not the real you. It simply houses your spirit. Although your soul is your personality, it is not the real you. For example, if you were in a coma, your soul would be unable to give expression through your personality. You would not be able to formulate and express your thoughts and feelings or make and carry out your choices. Nevertheless, you are still in there somewhere. The real you is your spirit man.

The enemy cannot approach your spirit or find the real you while you are dwelling in the shelter of the Most High. As you are dwelling, you can exercise authority over the enemy and protect your soul from the enemy's attacks. The enemy cannot approach or find your spirit man while you are dwelling because you have made the Most High your dwelling place. The enemy cannot enter a believer's spirit whether dwelling or not.[152]

When Psalm 91:10 says no evil will befall you, it is including evil as from the demonic realm. This evil will not approach you because you have defeated it.[153] Believers have been given the authority and the responsibility to defeat evil that comes from the demonic realm. Perhaps we would understand the verse more clearly if we paraphrased it. "No evil will befall you from the evil, demonic enemies you have defeated."

Paul was given a thorn in the flesh—an evil messenger of Satan—that had been sent by God. That thorn in the flesh was sent in order to keep Paul from pride.[154] In order to teach us things we need to know or in order to discipline us, God may send an evil spirit with a task to perform as He did with King Saul.

From a human perspective, there is evil we cannot control such as that which comes from tragedy, from other people, or from evil circumstances. However, in their spirit, dwellers will have the same resolve to serve the Lord as wholeheartedly as they had before the calamity struck.

From God's perspective, anything He allows to discipline us or to conform us more closely to the image of the Lord Jesus Christ is not considered as being evil. Concerning this phrase in Psalm 91:10, *Matthew Henry's Commentary on the Whole Bible* (electronic edition) says,

> There shall no evil befal thee; though trouble or affliction befal thee, yet there shall be no real evil in it, for it shall come from the love of God and shall be sanctified; it shall come, not for thy hurt, but for thy good; and though, for the present, it be not joyous but grievous, yet, in the end, it shall yield so well that thou thyself shalt own no evil befel thee. It is not an evil, an only evil, but there is a mixture of good in it and a product of good by it.

No evil will befall you,
Nor will any plague come near your tent.

If a Christian is not dwelling, the enemy can strike a blow to the soul or body that can indirectly affect the spirit of the nondweller. Psalm 143 says,

> For the enemy has persecuted my soul; He has
> crushed my life to the ground; He has made me
> dwell in dark places, like those who have long been
> dead. Therefore my spirit is overwhelmed within
> me; My heart is appalled within me. (Psalm 143:3–4)

How can this happen? Fleshly Christians operate from their soul, their body, or both. They are not operating with their spirit in control and are discordant with God's order—spirit, soul, and body. God desires that the Holy Spirit controls our spirit. Our human spirit is to control the soul. The soul then is meant to control the actions of the body. That is God's order. Therefore, the nondweller's spirit is in subjection to the operations of the soul or body and can be affected indirectly as a result.

A demon cannot *directly* affect a nondweller's spirit. The spirit is still the secret place of the Most High where the Holy Spirit sets up residence. Nondwellers might be compared to storm victims who are being thrashed about or injured because they did not take advantage of the safety provided by an available storm shelter during a violent storm. Because God dwells in a Christian's spirit, no demon would want to be in the nondweller's spirit, even if it could be. A demon has no need to try to draw nondwellers out of the spirit because they are already operating from their soul's own resources. Now the demon's goal is to convince nondwellers to believe and act upon the lies they have already been told. For instance, if nondwellers believe the words they speak do not impact their lives, they believe an untruth. James 3 is very specific.

> And the tongue is a fire, the very world of iniquity;
> the tongue is set among our members as that which
> defiles the entire body, and sets on fire the course of
> our life, and is set on fire by hell. (James 3:6)

Even though nondwellers may not believe the truth concerning the words they speak, their unbelief does not change the ramifications of that truth. Their words can defile and set on fire the course of their lives. The world, the flesh, or the future inhabitants of hell may influence those words at times. Concomitantly, if nondwellers are of the opinion that Christians cannot be influenced by a demon, they believe something that has no scriptural basis and may actually become a stumbling block to other believers.

If a Christian is dwelling, an enemy's attack may appeal to the soul or body, but that assault does not affect the dweller's spirit. The Lord Jesus Christ was a dweller, yet Satan's attack was an attempt to appeal to His soul and body through various temptations in the wilderness.[155] Christ's adversary was trying to convince Him to operate from the resources available from His soul.

"Nor will any plague come near your tent" cannot mean that dwellers will never physically or emotionally be plagued by disease or disaster. If that was true, it would be easy to tell who was dwelling and who was not by watching to see if they get sick, contract a disease, or experience any turmoil in their lives. If that was what the phrase meant, the Lord Jesus Christ would not qualify as a dweller because He certainly experienced physical and emotional turmoil both at Gethsemane and on the cross!

The phrase *does* mean that as we are obedient, God will not send a plague upon dwellers but will bless them.[156] He has promised to loose the plague against the disobedient and their descendants.[157] The Hebrew word for *plague* means "plague, stroke; wound … Each meaning carries with it the sense of a person "being stricken or smitten in some way."[158]

As dwellers are dwelling, the enemy will not be able to strike or wound the dwellers' bodies, although at times our souls or bodies may come under attack. Scripture does not promise that dwellers will never come under a demonic attack. Rather the Scriptures ensure that we *will* come under attack. That is why God provides His full complement of armor. If there was no possibility of a demonic attack, there would be no need for spiritual armor. Because dwellers know how to put on the full armor of God and engage in effective spiritual warfare, no demonic plague, stroke, or wound will come near physically. When they sense a demonic attack, dwellers have learned to take authority over the oppressive demon and force it to leave.

The demonic plague itself will not come near. The demonic attack that intends to bring a plague may be launched, but the plague itself will not befall dwellers. When dwelling dwellers sense a demonic attack, they counterattack and defeat the enemy, utilizing effective spiritual warfare tactics before the intended plague can come near. The enemy is baffled and confused. The lingering taste of dust remains as the aggressor's only reward!

During our stay on planet Earth, demonic forces will always be looking for opportunities to oppress us. It is our responsibility to resist these forces.[159] If an evil, demonic attack is launched, it is our responsibility to take authority over the demons as they attempt to deliver the plague by their own hand.

As a dweller, you have persevered and defeated an enemy's varied attacks. Therefore, the enemy that you have defeated will not be able to bring any evil or plague upon you. We will discover the reason for the victory as we examine the next verse.

Summary

**No evil will befall you,
Nor will any plague come near your tent.**

In this chapter, evil has been defined and illustrated through the life of Joseph. His life provides evidence that demonstrates the value of dwelling in the shelter of the Most High.

When this verse declares, "No evil will befall you," it does not mean that nothing bad will ever happen to the dweller or to the nondweller. Nor does it mean that no evil people or circumstances will come your way. We also found that evil is not necessarily what it appears to be. Evil from humanity's perspective differs when observed from God's perspective. It was noted that neither evil from within nor demonic evil would gain the upper hand over the dweller. We also considered the meaning of the phrase "Nor will any plague come near your tent" and discovered why that phrase holds true.

Notes

Psalm 91:11

The Angels' Commission

For He will give His angels charge concerning you,
To guard you in all your ways.

For He will give ...

"For He will give" is a promise the Most High has given to the abiding dweller. There is none higher than the Most High. The buck stops here, and He has decided, "He will give." What will He give?

For He will give
His angels charge concerning you ...

Speaking in reference to angels, Hebrews 1 makes this proclamation:

> Are they not all ministering spirits, sent out to render service for the sake of those who will inherit salvation? (Hebrews 1:14)

David Wilkerson's statement concerning angels could accurately portray Christians that do not dwell in the shelter of the Most High, but they may be quite familiar with the deeds of the flesh.

I wonder if the angels are baffled by all the worrying and anxiousness of those who claim to trust in God. To them it must seem so degrading, so insulting to the Lord, that we worry as if we had no caring Father in heaven. What perplexing questions the angels must ask among themselves: "Have they no Father who is in heaven? Do they not believe he loves them? Did he not tell them he knows all about their needs? Do they not know the Father sends us to take charge of them in times of danger? Do they not believe that he who feeds the birds and the whole animal kingdom will feed and clothe them? How can they fret and worry if they know he owns all power, all wealth, and can supply the needs of all creation? Would they accuse their heavenly Father of neglect, as if he was not true to his word?" [160]

The angels of Hebrews 1:14 are charged to render service to born again believers. The commission given to the Psalm 91:11 angels is expanded to guard dwellers in all their ways. This is not referring to what God will do for His people as a whole. Rather it is God's personal promise given to those who dwell in the shelter of the Most High. You will notice that the word for *angel* in this verse is written in the plural form. More than one angel will be given charge to guard the dweller.

When does God first give His angels this charge to guard the dweller? The Psalm 91 angelic guard is provided once you have committed to dwell in the shelter of the Most High and abide in the shadow of the Almighty. An angelic guard is then provided in order to guard you in all your ways. As they bear you up to keep you from stumbling, you will find yourself victorious in defeating oppressive, spiritual enemies as demonstrated in verses 5 through 7. Verse 8 reveals a truth that our spiritual enemies hope believers never learn.

You will only look on with your eyes and see the recompense of the wicked. (Psalm 91:8 NASB)

The KJV says it this way:

You will only observe with your eyes and see the punishment of the wicked. (Psalm 91:8 KJV)

Our spiritual enemies do not want dwellers to utilize the authority and power of the Lord Jesus Christ and thereby observe as demons get their just reward. Verse 9 gives the reason for that victory.

For you have made the LORD, my refuge, even the Most High, your dwelling place. (Psalm 91:9)

Potentially, all believers can appropriate the reality of God's angels guarding their ways. However, as we take the context of Psalm 91:11 into consideration, does God automatically extend this Psalm 91 angelic guard to all believers? This verse does not give that indication. This angelic guard is specifically there for those who dwell in the shelter of the Most High and abide in the shadow of the Almighty.

If we are following the ways of our flesh, we are not dwelling. Although God has given His angels charge over the dweller to "guard you in all your ways," angels have not been commissioned to guard the ways of our flesh.

A guardrail is used on our highways to keep cars within bounds or to restrain and prevent them from going into dangerous or unauthorized areas. The angels of Psalm 91 purpose to keep us within certain bounds and restrain us by providing specific instructions when we begin heading in a wrong direction.

- **Angels Give Instruction**

Matthew 1 gives an example of how angels provide instructions to a dweller.

> Now the birth of Jesus Christ was as follows: When His mother Mary had been betrothed to Joseph, before they came together she was found to be with child by the Holy Spirit. And Joseph her husband, being a righteous man and not wanting to disgrace her, planned to send her away secretly. But when he had considered this, behold, an angel of the Lord appeared to him in a dream, saying, "Joseph, son of David, do not be afraid to take Mary as your wife; for that which has been conceived in her is of the Holy Spirit. And she will bear a Son; and you shall call His name Jesus, for it is He who will save His people from their sins." (Matthew 1:18–21)

Notice that Joseph had considered sending Mary away secretly because she was pregnant and he knew he was not responsible for her condition. He had not yet made up his mind, but he was considering a course of action—a way to go. However, his logic or reason was not to be his ultimate guide. It was at that point that an angel appeared to him in a dream and gave him specific instructions on what he should do. Joseph wisely reversed his course and followed the angel's instruction.

- **The Prophet Elijah Receives Instruction**

The book of 1 Kings provides us with an example of how angels guard the ways of the dweller. Here we find Elijah challenging the prophets of Baal to a spiritual duel on Mount Carmel.

> "How long will you hesitate between two opinions? If the LORD is God, follow Him; but if Baal, follow

him." But the people did not answer him a word. (1 Kings 18:21)

Ryrie makes this comment concerning Elijah's question:

> *How long will you hesitate between two opinions?* Lit., how long are you hopping between two forks? Israel's sin was not that of totally rejecting Yahweh, but of seeking to combine His worship with Baal worship.[161]

Elijah continues by providing a detailed challenge to the prophets of Baal.

> "I alone am left a prophet of the Lord, but Baal's prophets are 450 men. Now let them give us two oxen; and let them choose one ox for themselves and cut it up, and place it on the wood, but put no fire under it; and I will prepare the other ox, and lay it on the wood, and I will not put a fire under it. Then you call on the name of your god, and I will call on the name of the Lord, and the God who answers by fire, He is God." And all the people answered and said, "That is a good idea." (1 Kings 18:22–24)

The prophets of Baal called upon their god with earnest sincerity, yet their voices went unheeded all morning. That afternoon, in frenzied anticipation, they used their swords and lances to draw their own blood as they continued to call upon Baal. Yet their god remained deaf, silent, and uncaring.

Once Elijah had seen enough, he called all the people together as he repaired the altar of the Lord, arranged his sacrifice, and had everything thoroughly soaked with water. After the preparations were made, Elijah prayed.

> "O Lord, the God of Abraham, Isaac and Israel, today let it be known that You are God in Israel and that I am Your servant and I have done all these

things at Your word. Answer me, O Lord, answer me, that this people may know that You, O Lord, are God, and that You have turned their heart back again." (1 Kings 18:36–37)

Elijah was not long-winded when he prayed, but his prayer received an immediate answer. The fire of the Lord fell and completely consumed his offering. The people immediately fell on their faces and said, "The Lord, He is God." Elijah then employed divine justice and slew the false prophets.

When King Ahab reported what had happened to Jezebel, she sent a message to Elijah that immediately got his full attention. Her words to the prophet are recorded in 1 Kings 19.

"So may the gods do to me and even more, if I do not make your life as the life of one of them by tomorrow about this time." (1 Kings 19:2)

Elijah apparently did not talk to the Lord about Jezebel's message, although he did respond to it. He immediately left on a journey that was induced by fear and the hope of escape. As Elijah was sleeping in the wastelands under a juniper tree, an angel touched him and instructed him to get up and eat the food that had been prepared. After eating, Elijah rested again. A second time the angel gave the same instructions. Once again, Elijah obeyed. It is not known what food the angel provided, but Elijah was strengthened by that food for the next forty days.

The angel appeared and ministered to Elijah by providing food and instruction that enabled the prophet to fulfill God's upcoming mission. Because Elijah was a dweller, the heavenly visitor redirected Elijah's journey and put him on the right path.

For He will give His angels charge
concerning you, *To guard you* ...

King Darius had assigned three commissioners to rule over his 120 assistants and was planning to appoint Daniel over the entire kingdom. The commissioners' primary function was to prevent the king from suffering loss.

The other commissioners and the king's assistants plotted against Daniel but could find no corruption in his life. Therefore, they approached the king and suggested he establish a statute that would forbid anyone in the kingdom to petition any god or man other than King Darius for thirty days. Anyone who chose to disobey the injunction would be placed posthaste into a den of lions.

Those plotting against Daniel asked the king to sign their document so that it could not be changed, which was in accordance with the laws of the Medes and Persians. King Darius chose to sign their injunction.

Even though Daniel knew the injunction had been signed into law by the king, he chose to continue his practice of praying and giving thanks to God. Once the other commissioners and assistants to the king witnessed Daniel continuing his practice, they went to the king, told him of Daniel's offense, and reminded him of the document that he had signed into law. Although it grieved the king, he had no recourse but to enforce the order and have Daniel thrown into the lions' den. Then he spoke to Daniel, saying,

> "Your God whom you constantly serve will Himself
> deliver you." (Daniel 6:16)

The king then retired to his palace and spent the night fasting. At daybreak he made a hasty trip to the lions' den. With a troubled voice, he again spoke to Daniel.

> "Daniel, servant of the living God, has your God,
> whom you constantly serve, been able to deliver
> you from the lions?" Then Daniel spoke to the king,
> "O king, live forever! "My God sent His angel and
> shut the lions' mouths, and they have not harmed
> me, inasmuch as I was found innocent before Him;

and also toward you, O king, I have committed no crime." Then the king was very pleased and gave orders for Daniel to be taken up out of the den. So Daniel was taken up out of the den and no injury whatever was found on him, because he had trusted in his God. (Daniel 6:20–23)

Daniel had been spared a terrible death because he trusted God. King Darius was pleased and commanded that those who had plotted against Daniel were to be thrown into the same den of lions. This time, however, the lions' jaws were not constrained by the angel, and the hungry lions quickly crushed the bones of the condemned men and their families.

God had sent His angel to shut the lions' mouths and prevented Daniel from being hurt by them in any way. Daniel was found innocent before God and was protected from certain death.

Although angels do guard God's people, whether dwellers or non-dwellers, the angels of Psalm 91 are sent to guard the ways of the dweller. Had the angel not intervened on Daniel's behalf, he would not have been able to continue on the journey God had for him.

For He will give His angels charge concerning you, To guard you *in all your ways.*

According to Deuteronomy, our ways are important to God, and His instruction is clear.

"Therefore, you shall keep the commandments of the LORD your God, to walk in His ways and to fear Him." (Deuteronomy 8:6)

Why would it be important for us to walk in the ways of God? God wants to bring His people into their spiritual Promised Land, where all spiritual and physical needs are abundantly met. If we refuse to walk in His ways, we will never find ourselves in our personal land of promise. Instead, like Joshua and Caleb's fellow spies, we will find ourselves afraid of the giants inhabiting the land. We will see ourselves as unwilling or unable to conquer the challenges that God sets before us and will live a life of want and defeat. To enter into God's Promised Land, it is imperative to walk in the ways of God. God promises that His angels will be on the job faithfully fulfilling their charge. The book of Deuteronomy underscores the importance of walking in *the ways* of the LORD.

> "And now, Israel, what does the LORD your God require from you, but to fear the LORD your God, to walk in all His ways and love Him, and to serve the LORD your God with all your heart and with all your soul, and to keep the LORD's commandments and His statutes which I am commanding you today for your good?" (Deuteronomy 10:12–13)

It is important to God that all the ways of the dweller are guarded. It is also interesting to note that dwellers are not required to ask for these angels to guard their ways. God simply supplies them. Satan is a counterfeiter and would supply his own angels to guard our ways. The book of Revelation says,

> 'But I have this against you, that you tolerate the woman Jezebel, who calls herself a prophetess, and she teaches and leads My bond-servants astray, so that they commit acts of immorality and eat things sacrificed to idols.' (Revelation 2:20)

Demons intend to work in such a way as to lead God's bond servants astray. The enemy would guide them along a destructive path leading to the ways of Satan where God would not want them to go. That is the opposite goal of God's holy angels. The angels of Psalm 91 are charged to lead a dweller in the ways of God.

The word *way* refers to a path or a route. How do Psalm 91 angels guard the ways of a dweller? An example is given in the book of Acts.

We find that the apostles and a group of Christians in Jerusalem were waiting for the promise to be filled with the Holy Spirit. The day of Pentecost had come, and Peter was emboldened by the Holy Spirit. As Peter began preaching, his words pierced the hearts of his listeners, and many were brought into the kingdom of heaven as a result. The religious rulers and elders of the people were up in arms concerning Peter and John because they had been involved in the healing of a lame man. As Peter preached, he was also proclaiming that Jesus had been raised from the dead. As a result, the Jewish officials had Peter and John imprisoned. Before the two apostles were released, they were emphatically informed they would not be allowed to continue speaking or teaching about Jesus.

Once they were released, however, the evangelists went to their friends, told them what had transpired, and they held a prayer meeting together. As a result, that group was also filled with the Holy Spirit, and they all boldly began speaking the Word of God. They were in such agreement that they began selling their homes and property and brought the money to the apostles who distributed it as was needed among the members. One couple, Ananias and Sapphira, found out the hard way that it does not pay to lie to the Holy Spirit.

The apostles were performing many signs and wonders around the environs of Jerusalem. The people were amazed as they witnessed not only people being healed but also witnessed the expulsion of evil spirits. The high priest and the Sadducees were jealous and had them thrown in jail once again. While imprisoned, they had an after-hours angelic visitor. The event is recorded in the book of Acts.

> But an angel of the Lord during the night opened the gates of the prison, and taking them out he said, "Go your way, stand and speak to the people in the temple the whole message of this Life." (Acts 5:19–20)

After releasing the Jewish leaders' captives, the angel spoke only eighteen words of instruction and left the scene. The angel's message, however, gave them heaven's marching orders. They were to continue teaching the Gospel of Jesus Christ. The angel had told them the way they were to go, and they did.

Once again, the Jewish leaders confronted Peter and the apostles. Their response reveals the impact the angel's message had made upon their lives.

> But Peter and the apostles answered and said, "We must obey God rather than men." (Acts 5:29)

Why would God have Psalm 91 angels guard the dweller in all his ways? He knows that the dweller will be involved to some degree in spiritual warfare. Because of the exceptionally deceptive manner utilized by the kingdom of darkness, a dweller's ways *need* to be guarded.

Although angels do battle the kingdom of darkness,[162] Psalm 91 angels are not commissioned to prevent demons from oppressing a dweller. According to James, that is our own individual responsibility as believers.[163]

The Holy Spirit teaches us what we need to know about spiritual warfare and enables us to successfully defeat our demonic enemies. Psalm 91 angels are commissioned to guard us in the ways the Holy Spirit has taught us and to keep those who dwell in the shelter of the Most High from getting off track.

Although this verse does not say Psalm 91 angels have other tasks to perform, in Elijah's case the angel's task included catering several nutritious meals.

Summary

**For He will give His angels charge concerning you,
To guard you in all your ways.**

The angels mentioned in the first chapter of Hebrews have a different commission than the angels of Psalm 91. The angels mentioned in the book of Hebrews minister to those who have inherited salvation. Psalm 91 angels not only provide specific instructions but also provide physical protection as shown by the life of Daniel while he was incarcerated in the lions' den.

Psalm 91 angels guard the ways of the dweller. After the apostles had been filled with the Holy Spirit at Pentecost, they became emboldened and began preaching to the crowd. The religious leaders took action and had them jailed. An angel was dispatched to set them free and then gave them their marching orders. Psalm 91 angels guard the dweller in the ways the Holy Spirit has taught during the course of the journey.

Psalm 91:12

They Will Bear You Up

They will bear you up in their hands,
Lest you strike your foot against a stone.

They will bear you up. When you bear people up, you carry them, you support them, you lift them up, or you encourage them in some way. Psalm 91 angels purpose to keep you in line with what the Holy Spirit has already taught you or is in the process of teaching you. Verse 12 expands the meaning of verse 11 by telling us *how* angels will guard us in all our ways. They will hold us up, support, sustain, lift up, and encourage us before we hit our head against a brick wall and can go no further.

In the last chapter, we saw an example of this when the jealous high priest and Sadducees had imprisoned some of the apostles. The angel opened the gates of the prison, released them, and gave them their marching orders.

> "Go your way, stand and speak to the people in the
> temple the whole message of this Life." (Acts 5:20)

The angel was not correcting any wrong behavior. The apostles were not off track. They had simply been forced to stop helping the people and were placed in jail by the religious leaders. The apostles were tied up, so to speak, and could do no more than witness, sing to the guards, or pray. That is when the angel intervened by freeing them and sent them back to teach the people about Christ.

After Jesus had undergone His temptation in the wilderness, angels ministered to Him. The ministering angels mentioned in Hebrews 1:14 minister to those who will inherit salvation. The Lord Jesus Christ did not inherit salvation. He *is* salvation! The Psalm 91 angels bear you up in their hands. It is their responsibility to carry, support, hold you up, sustain, lift up, and encourage the dweller.

- **Getting Off Course**

The Psalm 91 angels also bear you up when you begin getting off course or are getting away from the truth. Can a dweller get off course? If that were not a possibility, the present verse would not have been included in the psalm. Yes, dwellers can get off course, because they are not perfect. Elijah is an example of a dweller that temporarily got off course or off track. He had just called fire down from heaven, slain 450 prophets of Baal,[164] and outrun Ahab's chariot to Jezreel. Not a bad day's work. After King Ahab had related the day's events to his queen wife, Jezebel, she sent a messenger to Elijah to let him know she was going to have him killed the next day. Her threat sent him scurrying off into the wilderness with a death wish. It was while Elijah was depressed and running from Jezebel that an angel came, cooked him two meals, and sent him in the right direction because God had a mission for Elijah to accomplish. When a dweller strays from his position of abiding, the angels proceed to get him back on track.

Even though dwellers are abiding in the shadow of the Almighty, they have not yet learned all there is to know—nor will they this side of heaven. Therefore, even though they are abiding in the shadow of the Almighty, they can still make an emotional choice, or they can make choices without knowing the necessary facts. Thus, they have the potential to be off track and miss God's perfect will. Dwellers may also get off track because they are operating from their own resources or because they are uneducated or misinformed. If they are simply misinformed, they have listened to something that is not true and must be led into knowledge of the truth in that area. The angels are there to guard abiding dwellers in all their ways. They spring into action to fulfill their commission when a dweller ceases to abide. Otherwise, there would be no need for them to guard that dweller.

We have all seen parents of new toddlers hovering over their adventurous children, ready to support them as they take a few wobbly steps and to catch them if they stumble over their own shadow. You can almost envision the angels hovering around, ready to bear us up as we begin to teeter. The Psalm 91 angels are commissioned to bear you up in their hands. We are definitely in good hands with Psalm 91 angels.

They will bear you up in their hands,
Lest you strike your foot against a stone.

If you strike something, you hit it. The word *strike* is defined as meaning "to come into contact forcefully."[165] Psalm 91 angels bear you up in their hands to prevent you from forcefully hitting something that would cause you to stumble. However, angels are not celestial babysitters and are not concerned about us physically stubbing our toe on a rock or a stone.

A stone could represent something the enemy puts in your way to cause you to stumble or to trip you up. Satan's purpose is to deceive.[166] He wants his kingdom's forces to put something deceptive in your path that will cause you to move off your God-directed pathway. We have seen an example of this when Jezebel sent Elijah his obituary notice. Psalm 91 angels will guard against anything in the pathway that would trip up dwellers spiritually. They are commissioned to keep dwellers from stumbling and to keep them on the right path. Satan sends his deceptive, fallen angels to get them off track and to do the opposite of God's holy angels. Satan tried to do that very thing with Jesus during His wilderness temptations. Matthew 4 sets the scene.

> Then the devil took Him into the holy city; and he had Him stand on the pinnacle of the temple, and said to Him, "If You are the Son of God throw Yourself down; for it is written, 'HE WILL GIVE HIS ANGELS CHARGE CONCERNING YOU'; and 'ON *their* HANDS THEY WILL BEAR YOU UP, LEST YOU STRIKE YOUR FOOT AGAINST A STONE.'" (Matthew 4:5–6)

Satan knows Scripture and tries to use it to his own advantage. The tempter was telling Jesus that if He would take a flying leap off His high perch, the angels would bear Him up. Jesus did not give the temptation a second thought. Instead He quoted Scripture.

> "On the other hand, it is written, 'YOU SHALL NOT PUT THE LORD YOUR GOD TO THE TEST.'" (Matthew 4:7)

What does that mean when Jesus said, "You shall not put the LORD your GOD to the test?" Albert Barnes makes this comment:

> This is quoted literally from Deuteronomy 6:16. The meaning is, thou shalt not try him; or, thou shalt not, by throwing thyself into voluntary and uncommanded dangers, appeal to God for protection, or trifle with the promises made to those who are thrown into danger by his providence. It is true, indeed, that God aids those of his people who are placed by him in trial or danger; but it is not true that the promise was meant to extend to those who wantonly provoke him and trifle with the promised help. Thus, Satan, artfully using and perverting Scripture, was met and repelled by Scripture rightly applied.[167]

In other words, Satan was tempting Jesus to do something His Father had not asked Him to do. Had Jesus yielded to the tempter,

He would have been acting on His own initiative. He would have been operating from His soul rather than from His spirit. Had He succumbed to the temptation He would not have met the qualifications to be a worthy Savior.

Psalm 91 angels did not intervene when Jesus went through His wilderness temptations. Nor did God send any warring angels to fight off Satan. The battle was between Jesus and the tempter. In fact, the Holy Spirit had led Jesus into the wilderness so that He could be tempted. Because He was tempted, Jesus understands when we are tempted and can sympathize with us. Hebrews 4 says,

> For we do not have a high priest who cannot sympathize with our weaknesses, but One who has been tempted in all things as we are, yet without sin. (Hebrews 4:15)

Would the kingdom of darkness not use the same manner of temptation with believers today? Could we not be tempted to conjure up a plan of our own and ask God to bless it instead of following the plan God has mapped out for us? It seems that Ananias and Sapphira fell into that very trap. You will recall that they had sold a piece of property and had given part of the proceeds to the apostles to redistribute as needed. However, they had given it with the pretense that they had given everything. Peter told Ananias that Satan had filled his heart to lie to the Holy Spirit. Indeed, Satan had given Ananias the idea, but Ananias had made the choice to act upon the thoughts he had received. He then implemented a plan he thought would work.

Summary

They will bear you up in their hands,
Lest you strike your foot against a stone.

The Psalm 91 angels will bear you up. They carry, support, hold you up, sustain, lift up, and encourage. Certainly, that must have been the agenda when angels ministered to Jesus after His wilderness temptations.

Psalm 91 angels are there to do their part in keeping us on the right path and to keep us going the right way. After Elijah had confronted the prophets of Baal, his story reveals an angel's assignment once the prophet had gotten off course.

The Psalm 91 angels are on the lookout for obstacles the enemy may try to put in the dweller's way that would trip him or her up.

Psalm 91:13

You Will Tread Upon

You will tread upon the lion and cobra, The young lion and the serpent you will trample down.

You have made the Lord, the Most High, your dwelling place. The angels have guarded your ways and kept you from stumbling. Once you are stabilized in your spiritual warfare, God has a job for the dweller. That job description, which is also the heritage of dwellers, is given in this verse and assures our spiritual victory. Luke 10 provides an encouraging confirmation.

> "Behold, I have given you authority to tread on serpents and scorpions, and over all the power of the enemy, and nothing will injure you." (Luke 10:19)

Just as the Psalm 91 angels have received a charge, dwellers have also received a divine commission. It is the outcome of having made the LORD, the Most High, our dwelling place. Living out this verse is more than a declaration of war; it is *an act of war* against the original terrorists. Dwellers are no longer on the defensive trying to protect themselves or their families. They are now on the offensive and will be looking for an enemy to defeat. That is part of being on the alert after putting on the full armor of God. The victory is already there for us because of who God is and because of who we are through Him.

You will tread upon …

When you tread on something, you step or walk on that which you tread upon. As a dweller, you are commissioned to trample down the work of the enemy in your own life.

An example of treading on the enemy can be found in the book of Joshua. Here we find that Adoni-zedek, king of Jerusalem, was deeply concerned over the devastating defeat the children of Israel had been able to accomplish over their enemies at Jericho and at Ai. To complicate the king's concerns, the citizens of Gibeon had craftily made an alliance with Israel. Therefore, the king summoned four kings of the area to join with him in battle against Gibeon. The Gibeonites hastily sent word to Joshua, who responded by taking his army to the rescue. The words that the LORD spoke to Joshua were undoubtedly a huge comfort to him and his army.

> "Do not fear them, for I have given them into your hands; not one of them shall stand before you." (Joshua 10:8)

As Joshua came on the scene, God confounded the enemy and slew more of them with large hailstones than Joshua's army killed with the sword! There was more work to be done, but the amount of remaining daylight would not allow Joshua's army to avenge themselves of their enemies. Therefore, Joshua made a bold declaration in front of his men by commanding the sun and the moon to stand still. Astonishingly enough, that is what happened! Because God listened to Joshua, the children of Israel were enabled to successfully finish the battle with their enemies.[168]

The five kings that had joined to fight against Gibeon fled the battle scene and hid in a cave. When Joshua learned of it, he had the mouth of the cave sealed off and continued the battle. Once the battle was over, he had the kings removed from the cave.

And it came about when they brought these kings out to Joshua, that Joshua called for all the men of Israel, and said to the chiefs of the men of war who had gone with him, "Come near, put your feet on the necks of these kings." So they came near and put their feet on their necks. Joshua then said to them, "Do not fear or be dismayed! Be strong and courageous, for thus the LORD will do to all your enemies with whom you fight." (Joshua 10:24–25)

To some, Joshua's actions may seem more like overkill than a necessity. These were kings. They had been pulled out of hiding, forced to lie on the ground, and humiliated when Joshua's war chiefs put their feet on the kings' necks. Would that not teach them not to mess with Israel? Why not send them back home humiliated and let it go at that?

The answer lies in the last four words found in Joshua 10.

"Do not fear or be dismayed! Be strong and courageous, for thus the LORD will do to all your enemies with whom you fight." (Joshua 10:25)

We must be involved in the fight, and we must personally wage war against our spiritual enemies that intend to steal, kill, and destroy in our personal lives. Notice, too, that Joshua did not just slap the kings' hands and tell them to go away and leave Israel alone. No, Joshua then had the five kings hanged.

In reference to spiritual warfare, we cannot hang or kill a demon. However, we can destroy its work and take back any ground it may have acquired in our life before exercising our authority to make it leave.

You will tread upon *the lion* …

Psalm 91:13 tells us that *you* will tread upon the lion, not God. This verse should not be taken to mean we should physically try stepping on a lion. That would not be wise. The psalmist is using these terms to give a word picture that will help us understand the wide-ranging characteristics of the enemy that we will be opposing. Fighting this enemy is your privilege and responsibility as an abiding dweller.

It is a well-known fact that lions roar.[169] Lions are found primarily in Africa and roar for a number of reasons. A male lion will not only physically mark his territory in various places and ways, but he will also roar to announce his presence, to intimidate, and to inform any would-be challengers for miles around that this area is occupied. He is staking his claim for himself and his pride—the group of lions that live and hunt together. Since lions are nocturnal, they sleep a lot during the day and become more active as night approaches.

Although the males are very good hunters, it is generally the females in the pride that do the lion's share of the hunting. When the lions of a pride go hunting, it is a social affair. Some of the older lions wait until the younger hunters have stealthily surrounded their prey. Then they stalk forward in order to drive the proposed prey into the waiting jaws of those crouched in ambush. They often single out the weak or sick animals. When the moment is right, the hungry lions break out of their hiding and charge after their intended victim, whether it is an elephant, a zebra, a buffalo, or anything else that suits their fancy. A number of lions join in the attack as they grab, slash, tear, and bite. Generally, a lioness bites the animal's neck or muzzle and hangs on with the intention of cutting off the victim's air supply until it suffocates. Once dinner is served, the males—because of their larger size and strength—commonly bulldoze their way into the feast and aggressively run off any lion that tries to get in the way.

Lions do not always eat fresh kills. If a leftover carcass is discovered, the lions will feast on the remains of animals that have been killed previously, even if they must run off the original attackers that brought the victim down in the first place.

A healthy male lion is pretty much the king of his domain. Lions are eager to tear[170] into their prey and have no regard or compassion for their quarry. They will quickly kill for a meal. We would expect that from a lion since it is a wild, carnivorous beast in survival mode. Lions are bold and do not retreat.[171] They stand their ground and will defend their kill. A lion will growl over its prey and is not intimidated by the presence of a human attempting to scare it away.[172]

Although lions are large, strong, and do not have many natural enemies, their numbers are decreasing. Rival males wanting to muscle in on a pride will challenge and fight with the pride's dominate male. If the challenger is successful, he will take over the pride. Healthy lions as well as those that have been wounded in battle must at times drink from crocodile-infested waters, and they can become prey themselves as they quench their thirst. There are times when rogue lions will acquire a taste for human flesh, and thus, these creatures are signing their own death warrants. Humans pose the most serious threat to lions.

- **Demons Act in the Same Manner as Lions**

There was a time in the life of David when a lion stole a lamb from the flock while he was tending his father's sheep. David did not stand idly by but rescued the lamb. In the process, the lion turned on the young shepherd, and he killed it.

Demons act in the same manner as lions. Although demons may at times influence an animal, these spiritual enemies are primarily devoted to capturing and destroying people.

Demons will attempt to take and hold what does not belong to them, yet they claim it as their own. They will endeavor to capture one of God's lambs from His own flock in order to raze it. Demons are also bold. They don't retreat upon sighting a believer. If a demon has gained the right to influence an individual, it must be forced to leave, for it, too, will stand its ground and defend its claim. Although demons are eager to tear a person's life apart, they are not in survival mode. They are bent on stealing, killing, and destroying. They do so not for continued existence as the lion does but for their hatred of God and His human creatures. Demons, like lions, can be loud and threatening. The uninitiated can be intimidated and frightened when spiritual enemies do not cower and shrink from their voice or commands.

In the spiritual realm, far too many demons on the prowl have not been engaged in meaningful spiritual battle. Many Christians have no more than a mental awareness that there is even an enemy prowling about. Like a lion is his prime, demons do not have many enemies that cause them great concern. In 1 Peter 5:8, the apostle offers this warning:

> Be of sober spirit, be on the alert. Your adversary,
> the devil, prowls about like a roaring lion, seeking
> someone to devour. (1 Peter 5:8)

Your adversaries from the demonic realm are looking for someone to devour. Demons are aggressive, are on the offensive, and are looking for someone to harass and oppress. If given the chance, an unaware Christian may become its next target of choice.

The lion is known as the king of the jungle. In the spiritual realm, could this not represent a strong man as described in the book of Matthew?

> "Or how can anyone enter the strong man's house
> and carry off his property, unless he first binds the
> strong man? And then he will plunder his house."
> (Matthew 12:29)

The demonic strong man rules in the spiritual realm much like a lion rules in its physical realm. In the demonic realm, the strong man controls all other demons under its authority. He is the ruler of that group of demons.

On a larger scale, a very powerful demon stood against one of God's angels that had come to deliver a message to Daniel. Scripture says that this demon was the prince over the kingdom of Persia.

You will tread upon the lion *and cobra* ...

The king cobra, the world's longest venomous snake, is generally mild-tempered and would prefer to avoid humans, although it can become quite aggressive when provoked. If a cobra encounters a natural enemy such as a mongoose, it will try to escape unscathed. If necessary, however, it will fight any adversary it encounters.

The king cobra is well known for its system of defense and is equipped with enough toxic venom to literally kill an elephant. A king cobra's eyes can spot movement a full football field's length away. Its forked tongue darting in and out of its mouth can detect a victim's chemical information and direct the cobra to its next meal.

The king cobra's lethal venom is a special mixture of toxins loaded and waiting to be injected into the snake's next meal. If necessary, the venom is also readily available for defense against any would-be antagonist. A spitting cobra can spray its venom into a victim's eyes, which can cause much pain and temporary blindness. Within minutes of being bitten, the cobra's deadly venom affects a human's central nervous system, causing much pain and difficulty in breathing. Other toxins in the venom begin digesting and paralyzing the nerve centers that control the action of the victim's heart and respiration. If not quickly treated with antivenin, a healthy dose of cobra venom can result in death within thirty minutes.

When taking a defensive posture, a twelve-foot-long king cobra can raise its head along with one-third of its total body length in an intimidating pose.

A cobra can make a loud noise that sounds more like a dog's growl than a hiss, yet it can continue to maintain its aggressive stance in order to intimidate a perceived threat. With its forked tongue darting in and out between its half-inch-long fangs, its hooded neck fully expanded, its jaws full of lethal poison standing four foot tall with its round, beady eyes looking almost directly into the eyes of an antagonist, most human opponents should be adequately convinced that it would be wise to cautiously locate new territory.

When hunting, the cobra will bite its next meal and deliver its lethal venom. Once the animal ceases its struggles, the cobra will begin swallowing the creature.

Because a female king cobra lays her eggs among fallen leaves and guards them against predators, she can become quite aggressive as she protects her young. Even the cobra's self-sufficient young are equipped to employ their deadly venom as soon as they are hatched.

- **Demons Act in the Same Manner as Cobras**

Although invisible, demons can intentionally intimidate and try to stare you down as it examines you through the eyes of its miserable human victim. A demon's toxic venom resides in its subtle lies, which can stun the individual's desire to maintain a healthy spiritual life. A demon's venom attacks a person's spiritual vitality. The venom from one demon can poison many people.

When a demon injects its poison into a person's mind or emotions, it can cause great emotional pain and spiritual damage. A demon's verbal venom can cause spiritual blindness in its victim and paralyze the nerve centers of the soul, which interferes with spiritual heart action. Listening to the lies of demons is similar to being bitten by a venomous snake. Both instances interject poison into the system and can bring disastrous or even deadly consequences. However, an antidote can save a person's life. Although the antidote used to fight our spiritual enemies is God's truth, the demon's venom will continue its deadly work until the truth is applied.

Even though demons love to lie, a dwelling Christian who is abiding in the shelter of the Most High has learned to recognize and reject demonic lies. As a result, the dweller has become the demons' most dangerous enemy because the dweller will trample them.

You will tread upon the lion and cobra,
The young lion ...

Young, maturing lions have strong shoulders and stout forelimbs that are armed with long, sharp claws. Their powerful jaws are fitted with teeth that are quite adequate for killing small game and for scraping meat off the bones. When a young lion gains possession of a small animal to eat, it will growl a warning if one of its siblings comes near wanting to share its meal.

Can you imagine what might happen if a powerful adolescent lion were to find its way into a pen with a bunch of unprotected sheep? The sheep have no natural defenses against a lion's sharp teeth and claws. A young, healthy lion could easily kill some of the sheep if there was no one to intervene on behalf of the vulnerable sheep.

Young lions grow up and hunt together when they stalk larger prey. Even though dense cover provides an advantage, a lion will still crouch low as it stalks an animal in order to remain hidden from view. The Bible reveals the bravado of lions in Isaiah 31.

> "As the lion or the young lion growls over his prey,
> Against which a band of shepherds is called out,
> Will not be terrified at their voice, nor disturbed at
> their noise." (Isaiah 31:4)

- **Demons Act in the Same Manner as Young Lions**

What characteristics do demons share with young lions? When demons tear into one of God's sheep, they leave a path of destruction. Foul spirits will do all they can to target and destroy their victims' peace, their joy, their relationships, their marriage, their kids, or their finances.

Like young lions, demons also seek to hide and operate in stealth as they oppose the truth in order to weave their lies and deceptions in the hearts of their unsuspecting victims. The truth will expose the demons and make them vulnerable to defeat. That is why they hate the truth as they do.

Like young lions, demons will commonly growl a warning once you expose them and attempt to free their victim from their hold. Demons will do their best to protect those they claim as their own. They will use all of their available wiles to protect their victim from anyone who attempts to exercise authority and release the quarry from their deadly grasp. Demons commonly work with their evil associates in order to surround their victim and thus ensure a more successful campaign.

As dwellers who abide in the shelter of the Most High, we can either trample our demonic enemies or observe as they trample and tear the Lord's sheep before our eyes. Victory against our spiritual enemies is within the realm of possibility because Psalm 91:13 reveals that trampling them is the dwellers' privilege and responsibility.

> **You will tread upon the lion and cobra, The young
> lion *and the serpent you will trample down.***

Serpents can live in the mountains, in the desert, in rural areas, or in almost any place on earth with only a few exceptions. In the cold of winter, they will hibernate. Early in the day when it is cool, serpents enjoy lying in the warmth of the sunshine. When they get hot, they move into more shaded areas to protect themselves from the direct heat of the sun.

Many snakes (serpents) will remain motionless to avoid detection. Snakes such as cobras and rattlesnakes will stand their ground when threatened by an aggressor.

Snakes are predators. Venomous snakes must inject venom into their victim in order to kill it. After the venom immobilizes and paralyzes the victim, the snake simply swallows it whole.

A serpent can stealthily locate and quietly slither within striking distance of its prey. Its flicking tongue enables the crawling creature to smell its victim and hone in on its location like radar. Its camouflaged body colors blend in with its environment, making it more difficult to locate.

- **Demons Act in the Same Manner as Serpents**

Demons have access to every physical place on the planet. Unlike serpents, demons have no need for sunlight. However, demons detest being exposed by the light of the Son and desperately try to remain in the shadows of deception.

Demons are well equipped and masterful in their ability to avoid detection by those who should be the most reliable in detecting their presence. The late Keith Fredrickson, a counselor friend from Arizona, made this statement:

> The fact of creatures called demons and what they can do to people was established once and for all by the Lord Jesus Christ. Demonized people were found throughout the years of Jesus' ministry. Those events were recorded in the Christian Bible for all to read. Yet, Biblical evidence of demons seems not to be sufficient for many who are leaders in the evangelical Christian church. A pastor of a large Baptist church once said to me, "I don't know what I believe about demons." An evangelical Christian psychiatrist declared that in all of his years of

counseling he had never encountered a demon or a demonized person.[173]

In addition to avoiding detection, demons also inject their prey with poisons. A demon's poison comes in the form of lies, condemning thoughts, and negative feelings. Once applied, the demon awaits their toxic lies to immobilize their victim with disastrous effects. The venom spewed forth by a single demon can affect many people, leaving much destruction in its wake.

Unlike the lion, cobra, young lion, and serpent that operate in survival mode, demons are in a steal, kill, and destroy mode. Demons engage in their acts of terrorism to strike at the heart of God in an attempt to destroy and devour His prized creation.

The Bible refers to our responsibility regarding our spiritual enemies in Luke 10.

> "Behold, I have given you authority to tread on serpents and scorpions, and over all the power of the enemy, and nothing will injure you." (Luke 10:19)

Concerning the previously outlined verse, John Gill says,

> Which may be literally understood, as in Mark 16:18, or figuratively of the devil, and his principalities and powers, and all his emissaries, who, for their craft and cunning, and for their poisonous and hurtful nature and influence, may be compared to serpents and scorpions.[174]

Adam Clark makes this comment concerning Luke 10:19:

> It is possible that by serpents and scorpions our Lord means the scribes and Pharisees, whom he calls serpents and a brood of vipers, Mat 23:33, because, through the subtlety and venom of the old serpent, the devil, they opposed him and his doctrine; and, by trampling on these, it is likely that he means, they should get a complete victory over

such: as it was an ancient custom to trample on the kings and generals who had been taken in battle, to signify the complete conquest which had been gained over them.[175]

Revelation 20 provides good news for the Christian in reference to the serpent.

> And I saw an angel coming down from heaven, holding the key of the abyss and a great chain in his hand. And he laid hold of the dragon, the serpent of old, who is the devil and Satan, and bound him for a thousand years, and he threw him into the abyss, and shut it and sealed it over him, so that he would not deceive the nations any longer, until the thousand years were completed; after these things he must be released for a short time. (Revelation 20:1–3)

That serpent, Satan, and his kingdom will be thrown into the abyss for one thousand years to prevent them from deceiving people during the thousand-year reign of Christ.

Verse 13 of Psalm 91 tells us that dwellers will tread upon lions, cobras, and serpents. You tread with your feet. You cannot just walk on lions, cobras, or serpents without serious consequences. You must first incapacitate them. You must keep them from biting you, from running away, or from slithering off into the sunset. You cannot trample these enemies unless you overpower them. When you trample one of these adversaries, you are in an offensive attack mode.

What does it mean when your favorite football team says, "We trampled our opponent?" They are saying that no matter what the opposing team tried to accomplish, their schemes, plots, and attacks were countered and overcome. The home team trampled, overpowered, and beat the opponent down and then walked all over them.

Speaking of the Christian's adversaries, Psalm 44 provides this encouraging promise:

> Through You we will push back our adversaries;
> through Your name we will trample down those
> who rise up against us. (Psalm 44:5)

To *trample down* means "to tread heavily so as to bruise, crush, or injure."[176] When we deal with demonic entities, we are trampling a fierce, dangerous opponent that has no intention or commission to be stepped upon. You do not step lightly when you tread upon a demonic enemy.

• **A New Assignment**

As an abiding dweller, you have destroyed the work of your oppressive enemy. Now, however, there are new and greater battles on the horizon. Because God's angels have guarded your way and have done their part to keep you on track, you will be victorious as you put into practice what you have been taught by the Holy Spirit.

As a dweller abiding in the shelter of the Most High, you will engage your spiritual adversaries in successful spiritual warfare, even though these new foes may be more vicious than the ones encountered in Psalm 91:5–7. Regardless of the strength, stealth, threats, or poison the enemy brings your way, the dweller will walk all over his enemies and trample them.

Does Psalm 91:13 mean that dwellers will be directly involved in fighting or casting out demons at some point in their lives? It can mean that, but it may stop short of that and simply refer to an indirect involvement.

In the spiritual realm, our struggle is not with human enemies but with Satan's emissaries. In order to be protected, it is imperative we have an understanding of—and are clothed in—the full armor of God.[177] Once dwellers are dressed in their full armor they are told in Ephesians 6:18 to be on the alert for the saints. That is necessary because nondwelling saints may not be aware of or recognize their demonic antagonists. Those who do recognize their tactics must be on the alert for those who are falling at the hand of the enemy because of a lack of knowledge.

Consider the Great Commission found in Matthew 28.

> And Jesus came up and spoke to them, saying, "All authority has been given to Me in heaven and on earth. Go therefore and make disciples of all the nations, baptizing them in the name of the Father and the Son and the Holy Spirit, teaching them to observe all that I commanded you; and lo, I am with you always, even to the end of the age." (Matthew 28:18–20)

In verse 20, Jesus told His disciples they were to observe *all* that He had commanded them. The following verses in Matthew must be included if we intend to observe all that Jesus commanded:

> "And as you go, preach, saying, 'The kingdom of heaven is at hand.' "Heal the sick, raise the dead, cleanse the lepers, cast out demons. Freely you received, freely give." (Matthew 10:7–8)

In verse 8, Jesus commanded His disciples to cast out demons. I know of no biblical exclusion that allows for a lack of involvement in spiritual warfare at some level. Dwellers have the ability and commission to tread upon all spiritual enemies that come to oppress them.

At the very least, we are told to be on the alert for other believers. Dwellers would recognize the enemy and speak to those they suspect are demonized. As the opportunity expresses itself, dwellers could confront the enemy themselves, or they could point them to a ministry that knows how to scripturally confront them. They might help by directly supporting the ministry financially and with prayer. Dwellers may not be there physically during the battle, but they can certainly help encourage or enable the one in need to find help. Dwellers are part of the team, even if they are only working behind the scenes. Not everyone has the personality, time, or commission to confront demons head-on. We all have different gifts and callings. Whatever we are doing in the Spirit will be in direct opposition to the work of the kingdom of darkness. A dweller could be a pastor, a doctor, a teacher, a carpenter, a counselor, a janitor, a homemaker, etc. We can all tread upon the enemy by sharing God's truth to displace the enemies' venomous lies. Dwellers have been commissioned to trample down their spiritual enemies with truth regardless of their earthly occupation.

Summary

You will tread upon the lion and cobra, The young lion and the serpent you will trample down.

It is not until after dwellers have made the LORD Most High their dwelling place that they receive their commission to tread upon their enemies. Dwellers are no longer on the defensive, but now they take an offensive posture against oppressive spiritual enemies. An example of how a dweller treads upon his enemies was illustrated by the life of Joshua.

The psalmist used a word picture using lions, cobras, and serpents to describe the fierce characteristics of those with whom the dweller will fight on a spiritual level.

Psalm 91:14

Because He Has Loved Me

Because he has loved Me, therefore I will deliver him; I will set him securely on high, because he has known My name.

We have arrived at the point in the psalm where God speaks. The first phrase He uses concerning the dweller is, "Because he has loved Me." What does that look like? What message does this word *love* used in Psalm 91:14 provide? To answer that question, we need to see how it is used in other places in the Old Testament. In Deuteronomy, the LORD gave the children of Israel some instruction before entering the Promised Land. He told them to destroy the inhabitants of the land. If the heathen nations were allowed to remain, they would turn the hearts of the people away from the LORD. The children of Israel were to tear down their altars, destroy all their items of idolatrous worship, and burn their graven images. Scripture then records something very interesting.

> "For you are a holy people to the LORD your God; the LORD your God has chosen you to be a people for His own possession out of all the peoples who are on the face of the earth. The LORD did not set His love on you nor choose you because you were more in number than any of the peoples, for you

were the fewest of all peoples, but because the LORD loved you and kept the oath which He swore to your forefathers, the LORD brought you out by a mighty hand, and redeemed you from the house of slavery, from the hand of Pharaoh king of Egypt." (Deuteronomy 7:6–8)

Out of all the people on the face of the earth, the LORD chose the Israelites to be His own. He did not choose them because of any good of their own or because they were worthy to be chosen. In fact, they were quite obstinate and spiritually prone to wander. Rather the LORD chose them and set them apart as part of His plan. The *Africa Bible Commentary* makes this comment:

> The reason that Israel had to take such drastic action was that she was in a unique relationship to God. The Israelites had been *chosen out of all the peoples on the face of the earth* (7:6) and were now God's *treasured possession*. In case this makes them assume they are innately superior to others in some way, God hastens to remind the people that there was nothing special about them (7:7). They were an insignificant bunch, of no importance in world affairs. The only reason that God offered for his mysterious choice of them was that he loved them and was keeping a promise he had made to their ancestors (7:8).[178]

"The LORD did not set His love on you." The word for *love* in Deuteronomy 7:7 is the same word used in Psalm 91:14—*châshaq*. Strong's defines the word as meaning "to cling, that is, join (figuratively) to love, delight in, (have a) desire."[179] When the LORD "set his love," He chose to love the unlovely and the unworthy.

Other Scriptures are given that reveal another aspect of the Hebrew word *châshaq*. For example, the word is used when a man sees a beautiful woman, falls in love with her, and desires that she become his lawful wife.[180]

So in what manner has the one who dwells in the shelter of the Most High shown his love to his Creator? By using the Hebrew word *châshaq*, Scripture is saying that dwellers cling to, join, and truly delight in their God.

Do dwellers love God any differently than nondwellers? If so, how? Nondwellers may love God more for what He has done *for* them and might more commonly ask, "What can God do for me?" In John 14, Jesus made an interesting statement when He said,

> "If you love Me, you will keep My commandments." (John 14:15)

Obedience is a prerequisite to dwelling. Based upon the statement Jesus spoke in John 14:15, nondwellers do not love God in the same *manner* as dwellers do. That is not to say that nondwellers do not love God. They do. We can find an example of this in the life of Peter. Before Jesus was crucified, Peter declared that he would lay down his life for Jesus. Yet after His arrest in the garden of Gethsemane, Peter denied his Master three times.

After His crucifixion and resurrection, Jesus came upon Peter and some of the other disciples who had spent an unproductive night fishing. When Jesus told them to cast the net on the other side of the boat, they caught a net full of large fish. After Jesus had prepared breakfast and they had eaten, He asked Peter a question. He wanted to know if Peter loved Him more than the other disciples did. Peter said that he did. However, he did not love Him in the same manner that Jesus had asked. By using the Greek word *agapao*, Jesus had asked Peter if he loved Him in the same manner that Jesus's Father loved Him. Peter responded by using a word that meant he had a tender affection for Jesus. Did Peter love Jesus? Yes, he did but not to the depth he later demonstrated when the religious leaders threatened him. Peter chose to ignore their warning and obeyed God.

Nondwellers might say, "He saved me and rescued me from my use of drugs and alcohol. He rescued me from the dangerous situation I was in." Nondwellers tend to be more fearful of what God might require from them. Being apprehensive about what God might do *to* you or *with* you shows a lack of trust and reveals a lack of experiential knowledge concerning who God really is. Like the children of Israel, nondwellers may look to see the *acts* or deeds of God to determine what God is doing.[181] They look for physical signs as evidence of God at work.

Nondwellers may verbalize how they thoroughly trust God. Nevertheless, when trials come they act as though God is nowhere to be found. Their actions and their various verbalizations are not congruent. For example, they may say they trust God but then spend much of their time worrying. Such actions demonstrate that what comes out of the nondweller's heart deny and nullify the very words that are spoken. James tells us that works without a corresponding faith are dead.

On the other hand, dwellers say, "My God, in whom I trust." Their words and their heart agree, even though their circumstances are not favorable or may even be hostile. Dwellers love God more for who He is and have come to know Him experientially. Dwellers are more interested in knowing the *ways* of God.[182] Because the dweller's soul is not the primary organ of worship, a dweller worships God in spirit and truth. Jesus helps clarify the issue.

> "But an hour is coming, and now is, when the true worshipers will worship the Father in spirit and truth; for such people the Father seeks to be His worshipers. God is spirit, and those who worship Him must worship in spirit and truth." (John 4:23–24)

Dwellers have learned to worship in truth from their spirit. They are careful to put God first in their lives as an essential, uncompromising priority.

How have dwellers demonstrated their love to God? What belief, action, or faith has God seen lived out in the context of

Psalm 91 that would cause the God of the universe to declare that dwellers love Him? Dwellers have experienced God as their refuge and fortress. They have learned experientially that the Most High is trustworthy. Their knowing is not just academic or armchair theology. Dwellers do not trust God because someone else has told them He is trustworthy. Their knowing has been hammered out through their experiences on the anvil of life. Through experience, they know that the Most High is trustworthy, and they have chosen to do what He says. Dwellers have made the Lord their dwelling place. They have chosen to follow in the ways of God, and they do not fear their oppressors. Rather they dwell in the secret place of the Most High and confidently trample their spiritual enemies. Dwellers minister to the saints and thereby demonstrate their love to God.[183] Dwellers are willing to call upon the name of the Most High and put their trust in Him.[184]

There are two Greek words that translate as *love—phileo* and *agapao*. Phileo more nearly represents tender affection.[185] Thayer says phileo means to be friendly to one ... to delight in, long for, a thing.[186] In the book that bears his name, John talks about that kind of love. Mary and Martha were sisters, and their brother, Lazarus, had become very sick.

> The sisters therefore sent to Him, saying, "Lord, behold, he whom You love is sick." (John 11:3)

The word for *love* in verse 3 in the Greek is phileo. In other words, Mary and Martha were inferring that Jesus had a tender affection for Lazarus and delighted in him. They were friends. Instead of coming immediately to be with Lazarus, Jesus waited two days and informed His disciples that the sickness afflicting Lazarus would bring glory to God and that He also would be glorified by it. The story continues in verse 5.

> Now Jesus loved Martha, and her sister, and Lazarus. (John 11:5)

Verse 5 uses a different word than the one Mary and Martha had used in verse 3. The Greek word for *love* used in this verse is agapao. Vine clarifies the meaning of the New Testament word. The word is used as follows:

> In the New Testament (a) to describe the attitude of God toward His Son; the human race, generally; and to such as believe on the Lord Jesus Christ, particularly; (b) to convey His will to His children concerning their attitude one toward another, and toward all men, (c) to express the essential nature of God.[187]

When the Scripture states that Jesus loved Mary, Martha, and Lazarus, it is declaring that Jesus was expressing the essential nature of God toward them. Jesus loved them in the same manner that His Father loved Him.

After Jesus had journeyed to Bethany and met with Mary and Martha, He asked where they had laid the body. When they invited Jesus to go to the tomb, Jesus wept. Therefore, the Jews were saying,

> "Behold how He loved him!" (John 11:36)

Mary, Martha, and the Jews used the word phileo. By using that word, they were saying that Jesus and Lazarus were friends. They were fond of each other, and His tears gave evidence to that fact. However, Scripture declares that Jesus used the word agapao. He loved them. His love was not just a friendship type of love. Jesus loved His friends in the same way that the Father loved Jesus. In John 14, Jesus said,

> "If anyone loves Me, he will keep My word; and My Father will love him, and We will come to him, and make Our abode with him. (John 14:23)

Jesus said that if anyone loved Him, that person would keep His Word. The word for love in John 14:23 is agapao, not phileo.

The person who will keep God's word is not one who is just fond of Jesus or has a tender affection for Him and delights in Him. The ones who keep His Word are more than just friends. They agapao Christ. They love Him with the same kind of love the Father has for the Son. Agapao love is part of the fruit of the Spirit love that has become fused with our spirit. Regarding the Greek word agapao, Thayer says,

> When used of love to a master, God or Christ, the word involves the idea of affectionate reverence, prompt obedience, grateful recognition of benefits received ... denotes to take pleasure in the thing, prize it above other things, be unwilling to abandon it or do without it; to cleave to.[188]

Albert Barnes has this to say concerning the first part of Psalm 91:14:

> Has become attached to me; has united himself with me; is my friend. The Hebrew word expresses the strongest attachment, and is equivalent to our expression - "to fall in love." It refers here to the fact that God is the object of supreme affection on the part of his people; and it also here implies, that this springs from their hearts; that they have seen such beauty in his character, and have such strong desire for him, that their hearts go out in warm affection toward him.[189]

In John 14, Jesus said,

> "If you love Me, you will keep My commandments." (John 14:15)

The first part of the previously outlined verse is conditional. "If you love Me," meaning "If you agapao Me." The next phrase provides what will follow naturally. "You will keep My commandments." We might paraphrase the verse in this manner: "If you love Me, you will demonstrate that love for Me and will have an affectionate reverence for Me. You will promptly obey Me. If you agapao Me, you will gratefully recognize the benefits you have received, and you will take pleasure in Me. You will prize our relationship above all other things and will be unwilling to abandon Me or to do without Me. You will cleave to Me, and you will keep My commandments."[190]

Because he has loved Me,
therefore I will deliver him;

We need to digress for a moment and return to the first verse of the psalm to consider an important insight.

He who dwells in the shelter of the Most High Will abide in the shadow of the Almighty. (Psalm 91:1)

Once you make the choice to dwell in the shelter of the Most High, you are making a commitment that God will require you to fulfill. The first stage of learning to dwell involves appropriating the truths contained in verses 3 through 8. In those verses, dwellers experience the reality of being delivered from the snare of the trapper and from the deadly pestilence. They learn about seeking God's refuge and His faithfulness. They learn to take authority over their spiritual enemies and see them get their just reward.

Verse 9 reveals that those who made the choice to dwell have accomplished what they set out to do, for you have made the LORD Most High your dwelling place. A transition has taken place.

Verses 10 through 13 enlighten us concerning the ramifications of that choice. No evil will befall you, and no plague will come near your tent. Dwellers are assigned angelic guards and are assured they will tread upon some rather imposing enemies.

In verse 14, we run into the phrase "Because he has loved Me." Remember, the one who dwells in the shelter of the Most High will abide in the shadow of the Almighty. Verses 14 through 16 reveal what it looks like to abide in the shadow of the Almighty. In these last three verses, the promise given in verse 1 begins to unfold.

Our present verse, Psalm 91:14, reveals that obedience is not only a prerequisite to be delivered by God. Rather it is the assurance of it. Does God deliver dwellers differently than He delivers nondwellers? If not, these would be empty words, yet God does not speak empty words. God is saying that He will deliver the one who dwells in the shelter—the secret place—of the Most High. He delivers dwellers because they have demonstrated their love for the LORD by their words and actions.

In Psalm 91:14, the word *deliver* means "to escape, to cause to escape, save, slip away, to bring into security."[191] The psalmist uses the same word in chapter 31.

> In You, O LORD, I have taken refuge; Let me never be ashamed; In Your righteousness deliver me. (Psalm 31:1)

Referring to the righteous, Psalm 37 has this to say:

> The LORD helps them, and delivers them; He delivers them from the wicked, and saves them, Because they take refuge in Him. (Psalm 37:40)

With all their imperfections, dwellers are not delivered from trouble because they deserve to be delivered but because they love God and put Him first in their lives. The promises that God makes to dwellers are made because they love God. Because of that love, God promises to deliver them. In what way does God deliver them? He promises to set them securely on high.

Because he has loved Me, therefore I will deliver him; *I will set him securely on high ...*

What does God mean when He says He will set the dweller securely on high? The word *high* does not mean the dweller is placed in high heavenly places once the decision is made to dwell in the secret place of the Most High. According to Ephesians 2:6, every Christian is already securely seated with Christ in heavenly places. Psalm 92 says,

> But You, O LORD, are on high forever. (Psalm 92:8)

The word for *high* in the previously outlined verse refers to height, elevation, elevated place.[192] We could read the verse like this: "But You, O LORD, are on a high elevated place forever." That is not what Psalm 91:14 is talking about.

In 2 Kings 21, we are informed that Manasseh was twelve years old when he became king and reigned fifty-five years in Jerusalem. Moreover, he did evil in the sight of the LORD by rebuilding the high places his father, Hezekiah, had destroyed. He also erected altars for Baal and made an Asherah as King Ahab had done and worshipped all the host of heaven and served them.[193] The high places that Manasseh rebuilt were areas that were higher in elevation.[194] Psalm 91:14 is not talking about the dweller being elevated to higher ground like you would go to higher ground to avoid a tsunami.

> The LORD is high above all nations; His glory is
> above the heavens. (Psalm 113:4)

In this verse, the word *high* means to rise or to raise.[195] The verse could be read like this: "The LORD is raised high above all nations; His glory is above the heavens." Neither is this what Psalm 91:14 is talking about when it says, "I will set him securely on high."

The word *high* as used in Psalm 91:14 means "to be high, be inaccessibly high; to be (too) high (for capture)."[196] When Christians choose to dwell in the shelter of the Most High, God places them in a safe, strong place in which demonic forces have no access. The Spirit of God and the spirit of every Christian have been joined together at the point of salvation. They have become one spirit with Him.

> But the one who joins himself to the Lord is one
> spirit *with Him.* (1 Corinthians 6:17)

Demons are not allowed entrance into a Christian's spirit. His spirit is safe from their advances and attacks. When we dwell in the shelter of the Most High and abide in the shadow of the Almighty, it means God will place our soul out of reach of all spiritual enemies.[197] Dwellers will not be on shaky ground. Their footing will be sure because they are set securely on high. As dwellers, their soul is safe and strong in the LORD. Their soul is inaccessible to the forces of evil. They are securely abiding in the shadow of El Shaddai.

Because he has loved Me, therefore I will deliver him; I will set him securely on high, *because he has known My name.*

There are four Hebrew names for God given in Psalm 91:1–2 that reveal some of His various attributes.[198]

> He who dwells in the shelter of the Most High (El Elyon) Will abide in the shadow of the Almighty (El Shaddai). I will say to the LORD, (Jehovah) "My refuge and my fortress, My God, (Elohim) in whom I trust!" (Psalm 91:1–2)

God says He will set dwellers securely on high because they know His name. What does it mean to "know His name?" It means dwellers are gaining practical knowledge of the attributes of God and have learned to trust Him (verse 2). They have learned from experience that He is trustworthy.[199] David knew God experientially[200] as Jehovah-sabaoth, the LORD of hosts. Listen to David's heart as he speaks to Goliath, the giant that had taunted Saul's army in 1 Samuel 17.

> Then David said to the Philistine, "You come to me with a sword, a spear, and a javelin, but I come to you in the name of the LORD of hosts, the God of the armies of Israel, whom you have taunted." (1 Samuel 17:45)

David came against his enemy in the name of the LORD of hosts. Moses validates the LORD as a warrior in the book of Exodus.

The LORD is a warrior; The LORD is His name.
(Exodus 15:3)

Since God's character is revealed through His names, dwellers are warriors in the making as they learn to follow their Commander into their various spiritual battles. Those who dwell in the shelter of the Most High are taking on some of God's characteristics as their own, and in the process they are conformed to the image of the Lord Jesus Christ.[201]

Summary

Because he has loved Me, therefore I will deliver him; I will set him securely on high, because He has known My name.

Because dwellers have demonstrated their love for God, He promises to deliver them and to set them in an inaccessible, safe, strong place away from their spiritual enemies. Then God accentuates the meaning of His statement by declaring His reason for His action. He will do so because dwellers know His name—that is, dwellers have gained very practical, experiential knowledge concerning some of the attributes of God.

Psalm 91:15

He Will Call Upon Me

He will call upon Me, and I will answer him; I will be with him in trouble; I will rescue him, and honor him.

God is not speaking directly to a new dweller in this verse. Had He been communicating with a new dweller, He would have addressed him and said, "*You* will call upon Me, and I will answer *you*; I will be with *you* in trouble; I will rescue *you* and honor *you*."

Throughout Psalm 91, the seasoned dweller has been speaking to potential dwellers about the benefits of dwelling in the shelter of the Most High. After hearing the seasoned dweller's comments, it is as though God affirms what has been spoken to the group by interjecting guarantees that the seasoned dweller is not qualified to make and says, "Here is what I promise to the one who qualifies to dwell in the shelter of the Most High. Because he has loved Me, I will deliver him. I will set him securely on high because he has known My name. He will call upon Me, and I will answer him. I will be with him in trouble; I will rescue him and honor him."

He will call upon Me ...

Verse 15 gives one statement with four associated promises. The declaration concerning a new dweller states, "He will call upon Me." What does it mean to call upon the name of the LORD? When we call upon the name of the LORD, we rely and depend upon Him. We reach out to Him and have faith in Him. When we call upon the LORD, He is the focus of our call. He is not our backup plan. He is our primary focal point. We are calling upon the LORD, not something or someone else. In reference to salvation, Romans 10 says,

> for "WHOEVER WILL CALL ON THE NAME OF THE LORD WILL BE SAVED." (Romans 10:13)

The Greek word for *saved* means "to save, to keep safe and sound, to rescue from danger or destruction."[202] Who, according to this verse, will be saved? Those who call upon the name of the LORD will be saved. When we call upon the LORD for salvation, He is our focal point. He is our point of reference. We must look to the Lord for our salvation. Those who look for some entry point into the kingdom of heaven other than the Lord Jesus Christ fall into error as Acts 4 makes abundantly clear.

> "And there is salvation in no one else; for there is no other name under heaven that has been given among men, by which we must be saved." (Acts 4:12)

What Would It Take to Call upon the LORD?

- **The Unsaved**

What would it take to encourage a non-Christian to call upon the Lord? Sometimes it takes a national tragedy, a tsunami, a school shooting, a foxhole experience, or a life-or-death situation to cause an unbeliever to call upon the Lord. All too often when unbelievers find themselves in comfortable, agreeable circumstances, they tend to think that all is well and that they have no need for God. They may even consider such talk offensive or a waste of their time.

- **The Carnal/Fleshly Christian**

Why would a carnal/fleshly Christian[203] call upon the Lord? Although carnal/fleshly Christians are born from above, at times they may find themselves operating from a position of jealousy or strife with those around them. They may be very familiar with the deeds of the flesh and struggle with them on a regular basis. Although they may employ all the battle strategy they know, they commonly encounter more defeat than victory. They have not yet learned to appropriate the life of the Lord Jesus Christ into their daily walk. Carnal/fleshly Christians may readily call upon the Lord when they find themselves in some type of trouble, especially if they have been caught doing something they should not be doing or if they need or want something.

Carnal/fleshly Christians might also call upon the Lord after initiating a plan they want God to bless. As initiators, they can usually get things done on their own. Although they may trust their own abilities, at times they may feel they need a little extra help doing something. When they cannot quite pull off something on their own, carnal/fleshly Christians may ask for God's help. The prophet Isaiah speaks to the folly of depending upon anything other than the Lord.

> Woe to those who go down to Egypt for help, And rely on horses, And trust in chariots because they are many, And in horsemen because they are very strong, But they do not look to the Holy One of Israel, nor seek the LORD! (Isaiah 31:1)

The author of the book of Hebrews refers to those who are yet fleshly.

> For though by this time you ought to be teachers, you have need again for someone to teach you the elementary principles of the oracles of God, and you have come to need milk and not solid food. For everyone who partakes only of milk is not

accustomed to the word of righteousness, for he is a babe. (Hebrews 5:12–13)

Carnal/fleshly Christians are more accustomed to being spoon-fed and are satisfied with the uncomplicated elements of the Christian life. They may have little or no desire to press on into the deeper water of their Christianity where opportunity abounds for their faith to grow. Perhaps Moses fell into this category when he was making excuses as to why he could not lead the children of Israel out of Egypt as God had asked.[204] Conceivably, Peter qualified for this category when he purposed to prevent Jesus from being crucified.[205] Peter was looking at the situation from an earthly position rather than a spiritual one. He was operating from his mind and emotions as opposed to operating from his spirit. Figure 2 depicts the carnal/fleshly Christian.

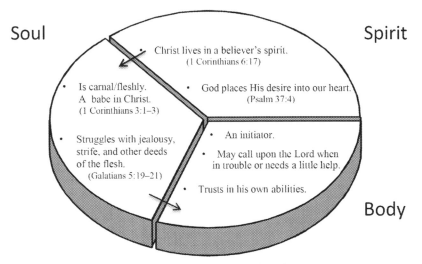

Soul

Spirit

- Christ lives in a believer's spirit.
  (1 Corinthians 6:17)

- Is carnal/fleshly.
  A babe in Christ.
  (1 Corinthians 3:1–3)

- God places His desire into our heart.
  (Psalm 37:4)

- Struggles with jealousy, strife, and other deeds of the flesh.
  (Galatians 5:19–21)

- An initiator.

- May call upon the Lord when in trouble or needs a little help.

- Trusts in his own abilities.

Body

Figure 2: The Carnal/Fleshly Christian

Another example can be seen as we look in on Zacharias and his wife, Elizabeth. Scripture tells us that God pronounced Zacharias and his wife, Elizabeth, to be righteous. Zacharias was a priest. One day as he was performing his priestly duties, the angel

Gabriel appeared to him, but Zacharias was troubled and gripped with fear. Listen to the angel's message, which is found in Luke 1.

> But the angel said to him, "Do not be afraid, Zacharias, for your petition has been heard, and your wife Elizabeth will bear you a son, and you will give him the name John. And you will have joy and gladness, and many will rejoice at his birth. For he will be great in the sight of the Lord, and he will drink no wine or liquor; and he will be filled with the Holy Spirit, while yet in his mother's womb. And he will turn back many of the sons of Israel to the Lord their God. And it is he who will go as a forerunner before Him in the spirit and power of Elijah, TO TURN THE HEARTS OF THE FATHERS BACK TO THE CHILDREN, and the disobedient to the attitude of the righteous; so as to make ready a people prepared for the Lord." (Luke 1:13–17)

Apparently, Zacharias had been petitioning God for a son to be born through his union with his wife. When Gabriel announced that God was answering his petition, Zacharias's mind went into action, and he questioned how an old man with a wife of advanced years could possibly have a child at their stage of life. His question did not arise from his spirit but from his soul. How do we know that? Notice that Zacharias was not concerned with whatever mission John might have in life; he was only concerned with what he felt were the limitations of the couple's aged bodies. His mind was centered on earthly issues, not heavenly ones. His mind would not accept what had already been placed in his spirit. Psalm 37 makes this declaration:

> Delight yourself in the LORD; And He will give you
> the desires of your heart. (Psalm 37:4)

Zacharias and Elizabeth had both lived their lives in a manner that was pleasing to God. One reason Zacharias had prayed for a son was that God had placed that desire into his inner man. His spirit knew the truth of the angel's message, but unfortunately, his soul and body were not listening to his spirit or to Gabriel that day. His soul was in charge, looked at his aged body, rejected Gabriel's message, and demanded an answer that would satisfy an earthly mind. Regardless, Gabriel did not accommodate the aged priest's fleshly question. Instead the heavenly messenger informed the unbelieving priest that he would be unable to speak until John was born. And so it was.

- ## The Spiritual Christian

Why would the spiritual Christian call upon the Lord? Spiritual Christians will call upon the Lord when they need direction in life and do not want to make a decision based upon human reason or understanding alone. It may be they need clarification concerning an issue in their lives. The story of Mary, the mother of Jesus, provides us with an example. God had sent Gabriel to Nazareth to speak to a virgin by the name of Mary. The heavenly visitor's conversation with Mary is recorded in Luke 1.

> And coming in, he said to her, "Greetings, favored one! The Lord is with you." But she was very perplexed at this statement, and kept pondering what kind of salutation this was. (Luke 1:28–29)

Mary heard the angel's salutation but was perplexed or troubled at what had been spoken. The word *perplex* is defined as meaning "to make unable to grasp something clearly or to think logically and decisively about something."[206] She was confused and could not make sense of it all, so she pondered the salutation in her mind. The KJV says it like this:

> And when she saw him, she was troubled at his saying, and cast in her mind what manner of salutation this should be. (Luke 1:29 KJV)

At this point, Mary's mind and emotions were in high gear trying to figure out what was going on. The angel reassured her and told her not to be afraid. She had found favor with God. The angel then told her she would conceive and have a child. She was to name this child, Jesus. Although Mary was engaged to Joseph, she was confused and needed some clarification. Her question to Gabriel was legitimate, and he took no offense because of it. Look at her question and at Gabriel's answer.

> Mary said to the angel, "How can this be, since I am a virgin?" The angel answered and said to her, "The Holy Spirit will come upon you, and the power of the Most High will overshadow you; and for that reason the holy Child shall be called the Son of God. And behold, even your relative Elizabeth has also conceived a son in her old age; and she who was called barren is now in her sixth month. For nothing will be impossible with God." And Mary said, "Behold, the bondslave of the Lord; may it be done to me according to your word." And the angel departed from her. (Luke 1:34–38)

This dialogue clearly shows that Mary was operating from her spirit, not her soul. Had she been operating from her soul, she may have thought, "Gabriel just informed me that I am going to be with child. However, I know that I am a virgin. What the angel's message means then is that since Joseph and I are engaged, we are going to have a son when we consummate our marriage. When our son is born, Gabriel said I should call his name Jesus. I cannot wait to tell Joseph the good news!"

That would have been a natural assumption on Mary's part and would have been a much easier, logical, and accepted explanation. There had never been an immaculate conception in the history of the world so that concept would not have registered in her mind. Another reason we can ascertain that Mary was operating from her spirit rather than from her soul is because of Gabriel's answer.

Mary did not question the validity of Elizabeth's pregnancy or insist on some kind of proof. After all, Elizabeth had been barren all her life, but now she was old! Mary's mind could have easily doubted Gabriel's statement concerning Elizabeth's pregnancy.

Mary also could have asked how the Holy Spirit would accomplish such an impossible task in her life. Modern science would ask the same question. No such thoughts registered in Mary's mind because she was operating from her spirit. Her spirit's function of intuition was in agreement with Gabriel's proclamation, even though her mind could not explain it. There was an internal knowing that what Gabriel had spoken was true. There were no more queries on Mary's part after her original question. She simply accepted what Gabriel had spoken.

There is another reason shown in Luke that helps us understand that Mary was operating from her spirit.

> Mary said, "Behold the bondslave of the Lord; may it be done to me according to your word." (Luke 1:38)

The Greek word for *word* is not *logos*. It is *rhema*. Rhema refers to that which is revealed to us by the Holy Spirit. Mary was so willing to accept Gabriel's message because the Holy Spirit had quickened her spirit to Gabriel's message. What Gabriel had spoken resonated with her spirit, even though her mind and emotions were reeling.

What is the difference between Zacharias's question, which was met with an angelic rebuke, and Mary's question, which was answered? The former originated as the outgrowth of an active, fleshly mind. The latter was the result of an honest question from her soul as she was seeking clarification concerning an important issue in her life.

Spiritual Christians have learned and accepted who they are in Christ. They have traveled further along the maturation curve spiritually than their carnal/fleshly Christian friends. The book of Hebrews sheds light on those who are spiritual.

> But solid food is for the mature, who because of practice have their senses trained to discern good and evil. (Hebrews 5:14)

A newborn is fed milk, not solid food. As the baby grows, it is natural to partake of food that has more substance. If children were forced to remain on a milk-only diet, would they have access to the nutrients necessary to develop physically strong, healthy bodies? No, they could easily suffer from malnourishment and be affected both mentally and emotionally. Many would consider a parent who kept an older child on such a diet unwise, and that parent might also be guilty of child neglect.

The same is true on a spiritual level. Salvation is the entry point to the kingdom of heaven. Every person entering that kingdom has received new life through the Lord Jesus Christ. Just as maturity is not instantaneous in the life of a newborn, neither is spiritual maturity instantaneous once a person enters the kingdom of heaven. Maturation is a process that requires time and proper nutrition, whether on a physical or spiritual level.

Although salvation is the essential ingredient to being born again, a salvation diet no longer satisfies those who are maturing in their faith. They have learned the ABCs of salvation and have moved forward in their quest for spiritual knowledge. Hebrews 5:14 tells us that solid food is for the mature. Maturing Christians are interested in solid food and have an ongoing desire to know truth. Once they learn a new truth, they store it in their arsenal of knowledge and put it into practice by applying it to their daily walk. By practicing the truth, they not only learn, but they are training their senses to discern the difference between what is good and what is evil.

The spiritual Christian and the dweller are more fully controlled by the Spirit of Christ, and both know who they are in

Christ. They are more mature than the fleshly and operate from their spirit, not their soul. In other words, they both listen carefully to and are guided by their intuition. They have a clear conscience and have meaningful communion with their God. They both utilize information that has been acquired from within their spirit rather than totally depending upon what their rational minds can understand. Consequently, their minds may not understand and may want to rebel against the desire of the spirit. Neither the spiritual nor the dweller make important decisions based upon irrational feelings they may acquire from their soul's emotions. Both the spiritual Christian and the dweller look beyond what their souls alone can offer and refuse to engage in haphazard decision-making processes. Because the soul interacts with the spirit, the spiritual Christian and the dweller are both in control of their body's actions. They walk by the Spirit.

Christians who are controlled by their spirit do not allow the body to do what it would naturally want to do that is in opposition to the will of God because of the knowledge they have acquired in their human spirit from the Holy Spirit. If, however, their spirit's intuition and conscience voice no concern, the body is allowed to act accordingly. For example, if the body wanted to engage in some unlawful sexual behavior, the spiritual Christian's spirit would immediately veto the body's request. The body of the spiritual Christian would comply with the spirit's decision. The body of the fleshly Christian might engage the sentiment of the soul's emotions and veto the spirit's demands by choosing to do whatever felt good without giving it a serious second thought. Figure 3 portrays the spiritual Christian and the dweller.

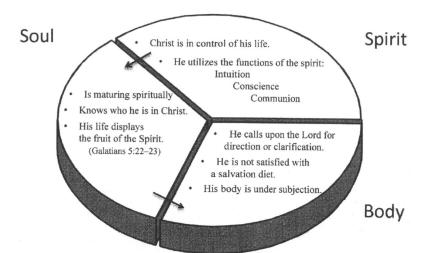

Figure 3: The Spiritual Christian and the Dweller

The terms *spiritual Christian* and *dweller* are not synonymous terms. Certainly, the dweller is a spiritual Christian, and all the aforementioned attributes are also found in the dweller. However, spiritual Christians may not be dwellers because they are not necessarily acquainted with the concept and responsibilities associated with dwelling in the shelter of the Most High and abiding in the shadow of the Almighty.

• **The Dweller**

Why would a dweller call upon the Lord? To begin with, dwellers have gained an experiential knowledge of the Most High, the Almighty, the LORD, and God.[207] In other words, these particular names for God are not just another way of referring to God. Each name of God reveals a different characteristic of the One the dweller has chosen to wholeheartedly serve.

Dwellers dwell in the shelter of the Most High and recognize that there is none higher. They acknowledge the Most High as the possessor of heaven and earth. They are assured that the Most

High will properly equip them for battle and that He will also deliver their enemies into their hands. They would not willingly allow anything to usurp the Most High's place in their lives.

Dwellers acknowledge that as the Almighty, El Shaddai is all-powerful and provides multiple blessings, both temporal and spiritual, to those who learn to trust Him and walk in His ways. They do not despise the chastening of the Almighty.[208] Rather they learn from it.

They are mindful that Jehovah, the LORD, is righteous[209] and therefore judges evil because it is contrary to His nature. Dwellers do not trust in the strength of their flesh but rather trust the Lord as they learn to disregard the whims and fancies of their flesh.

A friend loves at all times.[210] The first thing God acknowledges about the dweller in this psalm is that he loves God. When Abraham believed God, God counted him as righteous, and he was called the friend of God.[211] Dwellers do not call on God only when they are in trouble or want something. They call upon Him as they would call upon a trusted friend. They know He is dependable. By making the declaration that they trust in Elohim, dwellers enter into a covenant relationship with their God. Their natural response is to call upon their God whom they have learned to trust.

Four main characteristics reveal the differences between spiritual Christians and dwellers. First, dwellers have learned the importance of dwelling in the shelter of the Most High and abiding in the shadow of the Almighty. Second, dwellers recognize the reality, inevitability, and the responsibility of spiritual warfare. Third, they have learned to exercise authority over oppressive demons that purpose to ensnare them. Fourth, they are also on the alert for fellow believers that are not aware of how their enemies conspire against them.

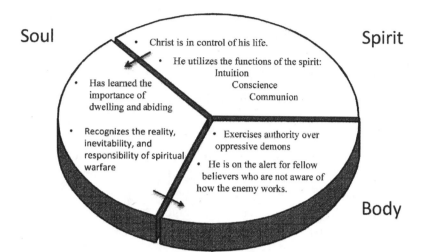

Soul

Spirit

Body

- Christ is in control of his life.
- He utilizes the functions of the spirit:
  Intuition
  Conscience
  Communion
- Has learned the importance of dwelling and abiding
- Recognizes the reality, inevitability, and responsibility of spiritual warfare
- Exercises authority over oppressive demons
- He is on the alert for fellow believers who are not aware of how the enemy works.

Figure 4: The Dweller

- **Elijah**

Dwellers have learned that the LORD oftentimes implants His own desire into the heart.[212] Since they understand the LORD initiated the aspiration, dwellers are assured the LORD will answer the cry of their heart when they call upon Him. As an example of the LORD initiating something in the life of a dweller, we could consider Elijah's grand debut in 1 Kings 17.

> Now Elijah the Tishbite, who was of the settlers of Gilead, said to Ahab, "As the LORD, the God of Israel lives, before whom I stand, surely there shall be neither dew nor rain these years, except by my word." (1 Kings 17:1)

Why would King Ahab's kingdom experience a drought, and why would a prophet of God be involved?[213] Drought was one of the punishments promised to those who forsook the LORD. King Ahab had done just that by doing more evil than all the preceding kings of Israel. To make matters worse, he married Jezebel, who served and worshipped Baal. He erected an altar for Baal, built the god a house, and made an Asherah—an image of a Phoenician goddess that was associated with Baal and lewd worship.[214]

When Elijah confronted King Ahab, he declared that there would be no dew or rain unless the prophet said there would be. That was a rather bold statement. Most weather forecasters would have no difficulty finding that to be a bold statement, even if they lived in a desert! If God had not given the message to Elijah, how would the prophet know what to say, or how would he know if what he said would come to pass if he did say it? He had to completely trust in the One giving the message—and Elijah did. In 1 Kings 18, we find another message given to Elijah that had been initiated by the LORD.

> Now it happened after many days that the word of
> the LORD came to Elijah in the third year, saying,
> "Go, show yourself to Ahab, and I will send rain on
> the face of the earth." (1 Kings 18:1)

Is it possible that Elijah did not hear these words audibly but rather perceived them in his spirit? Is that not how it usually works now? You may remember that communion is a function of the spirit, not the soul. At any rate, God was the initiator of the drought and the rain, not Elijah.

The word *initiate* means "to cause or facilitate the beginning of."[215] If a man operates on his own initiative, it means that he originates something. What you initiate starts with you, the initiator. Jesus, the Son of the Most High, did not operate on His own initiative. John 5 records Jesus's own statement.

> "I can do nothing on My own initiative. As I hear,
> I judge; and My judgment is just, because I do not
> seek My own will, but the will of Him who sent Me."
> (John 5:30)

Jesus did nothing on His own initiative. Neither did Elijah initiate either message to Ahab. The prophet's responsibility was to deliver the messages he had received to King Ahab.

For three and a half years, the land had seen no dew or rain. The drought was so severe that King Ahab and Obadiah, the governor of Ahab's household, were searching the land for grass to feed the horses, mules, and cattle. During Obadiah's search, Elijah met up with the governor and instructed him to locate the king and to inform him where he could find Elijah.

Once King Ahab made contact with Elijah, the king accused him of being the cause of Israel's trouble. Elijah did not back down but told the angry king that Israel's trouble came as a result of the king's own sin and those of his ancestors who had abandoned the commandments of the LORD. He then instructed King Ahab to gather all of Israel and the 450 prophets of Baal at Mount Carmel. There the true God would be identified.

Once everyone was in place, Elijah set the parameters for the upcoming test. After giving the false prophets ample opportunity to hear from their god, the validity of Elijah's faith was tested and proved as he called upon the LORD.

Promise #1

I Will Answer Him.

"I am He the One who knows this dweller. I have revealed Myself to him, and I will answer him." God is waiting for the dweller to call upon Him so He can answer him.

Returning to the incident on Mount Carmel, we find that the LORD's answer to Elijah's prayer did not delay in coming. Rather His answer was immediate, spectacular, and effective.

> Then the fire of the LORD fell and consumed the burnt offering and the wood and the stones and the dust, and licked up the water that was in the trench. When all the people saw it, they fell on their faces;

and they said, "The LORD, He is God; the LORD, He is God." (1 Kings 18:38–39)

Elijah's prayer to his faithful God was quickly answered much to the dismay of the false prophets who paid with their lives. There are times, however, when God chooses not to answer.

- **God Does Not Answer Those Who Are Disobedient.**

You may recall that God had given the land of the Amorites to the children of Israel. All God required of His people was to overrun their enemies, destroy them, and take possession of their land. However, the children of Israel wanted to search out the land before going in, and Moses approved their plan. Unfortunately, that plan resulted in their downfall. Although they did search out the land and found it to be a good land full of promise, they discovered the land also contained men of great stature, and they became fearful. As a result, they grumbled and rebelled against the command of God. They even accused God of hating them and wanting to cause their demise at the hand of the Amorites.

Even though Moses, Caleb, and Joshua assured the people that God would fight for them, they rebelled by refusing to take possession of the land. They naively voiced their concern that their children would become the prey of the land's fearsome inhabitants. Their bottom line reveals that they did not trust God. They looked at their circumstances through the eyes of their own mental reasoning and came to the conclusion that it would be suicidal to try to follow the command of God. Therefore, they refused. Their decision did not set well with God. He declared that the rebels would never see the Promised Land. He would give it to their children. After some time of rethinking their position, they initiated a plan of their own and decided it would be an easy thing to go ahead and take possession of the land. Although they dressed in preparation for war, God would not be going with them. Moses warned them not to go, but they had made their decision. They would take the land by force.

True to His word, the LORD did not go with the confident rebels or fight for them. Thus, the children of Israel were defeated before their enemies, and Moses documented the result.

> "Then you returned and wept before the LORD; but the LORD did not listen to your voice, nor give ear to you." (Deuteronomy 1:45)

In the psalm under consideration, God promises to answer the dweller, not those who are disobedient.

- **God Does Not Answer when We Believe Lies about Him.**

The book of Job testifies to the fact that God does not answer when we believe lies about Him. As Job was going through all of his difficult times (which were initiated by God and tested by Satan), he recklessly vented his thoughts toward his Maker. His attitude is revealed in the book that bears his name.

> "He has cast me into the mire, And I have become like dust and ashes. I cry out to You for help, but You do not answer me; I stand up, and You turn Your attention against me." (Job 30:19–20)

Job's reaction was based upon what had taken place in the physical realm, and he had come to his conclusions from within the context of his own mind and emotions. Neither his mind nor his emotions had accepted truth from his spirit. Had that been true, Job would have realized God was at work in his life, revealing an area of weakness and falseness. Later we find that Job wisely acknowledged that pity parties do not move God.

> "Surely God will not listen to an empty cry, nor will the Almighty regard it." (Job 35:13)

Although some people may find a measure of success by organizing a pity party, we cannot expect God to answer us when we are having an emotional temper tantrum. Scripture also informs us that when we allow wickedness to remain in our heart, God will not listen to us.[216] In other words, if I am believing and acting upon lies or intentionally allowing some sin to reign in my life, I have no right to expect God to listen to my pleas for help or to provide an answer to my query.

- **God Does Not Answer during a Test.**

It is a common practice among teachers at all levels to spring tests upon their students to find out how much they have learned during a course of study. During a test a teacher is not required or expected to provide answers. Rather students are expected to respond in such a way as to demonstrate their knowledge of the subject being tested.

In like manner, once God has revealed truth to us, He will allow a situation or circumstance to come our way that will determine whether or not we will act according to what He has revealed or if we will revert to the destructive ways of the flesh. It will also reveal whether or not we listen to the lies of the enemy or if we determine to believe what God has spoken.

During a time of testing, God is commonly silent. He is giving time for those being tested to demonstrate what they really believe by their actions. For instance, people may say they trust God, yet when adversity knocks on their door, their actions do not line up with what they have been saying. In order for our faith to be more precious than gold, it must pass the test of adversity. The dweller's faith has been tested and found to be true.

Promise #2

I Will Be with Him in Trouble.

When Elijah spoke to King Ahab, he spoke as one in authority. He did not *ask* the king to cooperate. Elijah expected the king to follow his instructions. Speaking to a king in that manner was not the healthiest thing a person could do. Ahab had also accused Elijah of being the cause of Israel's drought. In addition, Elijah was grossly outnumbered when he challenged and intimidated Jezebel's prophets.

Look at the second promise that God makes to the dweller in this verse, "I will be with him in trouble." Dwellers can be assured that when they encounter trouble, distress, or a severe dilemma, God will be right there to stand with them. When dwellers are unable to rid themselves of a particular trouble or to find its cure, God has promised to come to their rescue.

The word *trouble* means "adversity, affliction, anguish, distress, or tribulation."[217] Deep trouble commonly has a way of causing people to aggressively seek the Lord. There are times, however, when God hides Himself during troubling times. It is not because God fears the trouble we are in. Nor is it because He knows He can do nothing about it. Rather it is because He is forcing us to come to grips with various issues in our life. Psalm 10 expresses the concern of many who find themselves in the midst of a troubling, trying situation.

> Why do You stand afar off, O LORD? Why do You
> hide Yourself in times of trouble? (Psalm 10:1)

God has promised that He will never leave us or forsake us. Yet when trouble hits, we sometimes form an opinion that God has done just that. Such a time as that is an opportunity for the enemy to come in like a flood and try to inundate us with negative thoughts and feelings. It is also an opportunity to practice taking our thoughts captive to the obedience of Christ. It is good to be reminded of the wisdom found in Romans 8.

> And we know that God causes all things to work
> together for good to those who love God, to those
> who are called according to His purpose. (Romans
> 8:28)

This verse is not telling us that everything that happens to us is good. It is saying that in some way we may not understand at the time, God can cause even the bad things to work for our good. We saw an example of this in our study of Job.

There are also times when God *creates* trouble in order to get people's attention. Then He teaches them as they go through it. The book of Jonah provides a compelling illustration in the first chapter. God had instructed Jonah to report to Nineveh with specific instructions to follow once he arrived in the target city. Jonah, however, had a variant opinion and headed for Tarshish to escape from the LORD. En route, Jonah's getaway vessel ran into very turbulent seas. God's wayward messenger knew he was the cause of the horrendous storm and recommended the sailors throw him into the raging sea. In an effort to save themselves and their ship, the crew followed Jonah's strange advice. The result was astounding. The sea became calm, but Jonah found himself surrounded in trouble. He would never have believed the event had he not been there to witness it. The book of Jonah provides the detail.

> And the LORD appointed a great fish to swallow
> Jonah, and Jonah was in the stomach of the fish
> three days and three nights. (Jonah 1:17)

During Jonah's submarine-like aquatic adventure, he had a change of heart and a change of plans. At that point, God commanded that great fish to deliver Jonah onto the seashore. When the itinerant preacher's feet hit the sandy beach, he was headed posthaste for Nineveh! God had created a troubling situation for Jonah, one that required his full and immediate attention!

At other times God is found to be a stronghold in times of trouble. Psalm 9 says,

> The LORD also will be a stronghold for the oppressed,
> a stronghold in times of trouble. (Psalm 9:9)

A stronghold is a lofty or inaccessible place. The LORD is that stronghold, and He is always there when trouble strikes. The dweller can also take comfort from Psalm 27.

> For in the day of trouble He will conceal me in His tabernacle; In the secret place of His tent He will hide me; He will lift me up on a rock. (Psalm 27:5)

In verse 15 of Psalm 91, God did not say He would remove trouble from dwellers. He promised to be with them while they are in the midst of their trouble. When a dweller calls upon God, He will answer because a two-way spiritual communication has been established. In times of trouble, God will be with him and will personally rescue him.

Promise #3

I Will Rescue Him.

This is the ultimate search and rescue operation. Any time God begins a rescue, it is more than just a hopeful attempt. It is certain to succeed. God promises to rescue the one who loves Him. What does it mean to be rescued by God? Rather than saying, "I will rescue him," the King James Version uses the phrase "I will deliver him." One meaning of the word in the Hebrew language means "to equip (for war), to arm for war."[218] An example of this usage is found in Numbers 31.

> Then the LORD spoke to Moses, saying, "Take full vengeance for the sons of Israel on the Midianites; afterward you will be gathered to your people." Moses spoke to the people, saying, "Arm men from

among you for the war, that they may go against Midian, to execute the Lord's vengeance on Midian." (Numbers 31:1–3)

When Moses told the people to "arm men", he meant they were to equip and prepare themselves for war. When an army is properly equipped, it has the equipment, intelligence, ability, and training it needs to defeat an opposing enemy. Therefore, when God says He will rescue the dweller, He is talking about equipping and enabling the dweller to completely defeat all enemy forces that may oppose him.

We need to investigate another meaning. Consider the following sentence that makes use of the word *rescue*: After the crash of their military helicopter in enemy territory, the crew found themselves in need of rescue. In the preceding sentence, the word *rescue* carries the connotation that those involved in the helicopter crash were unable to remove themselves from their precarious situation. They were in need of rescue.

In verse 14 of Psalm 91, we find that God had already delivered the dweller and set him on high—in an inaccessible, safe, and strong place. In this place the dweller has communion with God, and God promises to answer. God is even with him in troubling situations. Psalm 18 says,

> He made darkness his secret place; his pavilion round about him were dark waters and thick clouds of the skies. (Psalm 18:11 KJV)

Darkness is another hiding place, shelter, or secret place of the Most High. Strong's word for *secret place* is the same word that is used in Psalm 91:1. "He who dwells in the secret place of the Most High." In other words, God is with the dweller even when He has him or her in a dark place devoid of understanding. Now in verse 15, God says, "I will rescue him." Rescue him from what?

Psalm 91:15 is not referring to dwellers who by their own doing get themselves in trouble so deep that God has to intervene. How do we know this? In verse 11, we have seen how God's angels had previously been sent to guard the dweller in all his ways. In verse 13, the dweller has already successfully trod upon his enemies. He is not in any self-made kind of trouble because of poor judgment. Nor is he in trouble because of his spiritual enemies. God has even delivered him and placed him in an inaccessible, safe, and strong place. So what does the dweller need to be rescued from?

In verse 2, the dweller makes the statement that his trust is in God. When God leads a dweller to step out in faith and trust Him even when it makes no sense, it won't be long before the dweller uses up his own resources and needs a divine rescue. The dweller is not initiating a plan that he is asking God to bless. This refers to a plan that comes from a God-given desire of the heart. Dwellers are required to move in faith past their own logic and reason in order to be placed in a situation requiring the hand of God to provide a much-needed rescue. God will perform a divine rescue and will strengthen the dweller's faith in the process.

The story of Joseph is a case in point. As a teenager, God had given him two dreams that he shared with his family. Because of his brothers' jealousy and hatred for him, they considered killing him. Instead they sold him to some Midianite traders who took him to Egypt. There they sold him to Potiphar, Pharaoh's officer. Joseph found favor with Potiphar and became his personal servant. In the course of events, he was falsely accused of sexual misconduct by Potiphar's wife and was imprisoned. While in jail, God gave him favor with the chief jailer. God also gave him the interpretation for the dreams that Pharaoh's cupbearer and baker had dreamed. Although Joseph's interpretation of the dreams were accurate and came to pass, the chief cupbearer forgot him. Consequently, Joseph remained in jail for two more years. Then Pharaoh had a dream that his staff was unable to interpret, so the chief cupbearer told Pharaoh that Joseph could interpret dreams. Pharaoh sent for Joseph, and he interpreted the dream correctly.

The hand of God was upon Joseph from the beginning. Although his brothers' actions against him were evil, God meant it for good. In the end, God rescued Joseph and he even became a ruler of Egypt second to Pharaoh himself. God had rescued Joseph out of a situation from which he could not extract himself.

Promise #4

I Will Rescue Him *and Honor Him*.

We find that God did honor Elijah and find this report logged in his honor in the book of James.

> The effective prayer of a righteous man can accomplish much. Elijah was a man with a nature like ours, and he prayed earnestly that it would not rain; and it did not rain on the earth for three years and six months. And he prayed again, and the sky poured rain and the earth produced its fruit. (James 5:16–18)

When we honor a person, it means we treat them with respect and esteem. An example is provided in the following sentence: The brave police officer was honored because he rescued a fellow officer who had been severely wounded. In that sentence, the police officer was honored because of his actions.

However, getting into situations where they need to be rescued does not normally honor people. You would probably not hear this on the evening news: "We are here to honor Jack today because he was rebelliously skiing in an unauthorized zone. Although he survived being buried alive by an avalanche, his action precipitated the death of four other skiers. We honor Jack today for his adventuresome spirit." Jack may make the news, but he should not be honored for his actions!

As a king was always honored after his victory in war, so will the dweller be honored as being "more than a conqueror."[219] What does it mean to be honored by God? Peter sheds some light for us in the first chapter of his first book.

> In this you greatly rejoice, even though now for a little while, if necessary, you have been distressed by various trials, so that the proof of your faith, being more precious than gold which is perishable, even though tested by fire, may be found to result in praise and glory and honor at the revelation of Jesus Christ. (1 Peter 1:6–7)

Peter is telling us we go through these various trials as proof of our faith. We are told that faith is of greater value than gold. Although gold is perishable, true faith is not. It is our faith that is on trial and must withstand the acid test of adversity. Adversity establishes the validity of our faith. True faith that has been proven will result in praise, glory, and honor when Christ is revealed. Those who honor God will receive honor from God.[220]

John reveals what occurs when we serve Christ.

> "If anyone serves Me, he must follow Me; and where I am, there My servant will be also; if anyone serves Me, the Father will honor him." (John 12:26)

What does it mean to serve? To *serve* can mean to be ready and prepared to offer food and drink to the guests to fulfill a need or desire. It can also mean to supply food and the necessities of life. The word for *serve* is the same word used in Matthew 4:11 when the angels "ministered" to Jesus after being tempted by the devil. The angels were there to do His bidding without question, grumbling, deviation, or hesitation. One who serves the Lord must do the same.

The apostle Peter tells us how God honored Jesus at His transfiguration.

For when He received honor and glory from God the Father, such an utterance as this was made to Him by the Majestic Glory, "This is My beloved Son with whom I am well-pleased" — (2 Peter 1:17)

When Jesus heard His Father say, "This is My beloved Son with whom I am well-pleased" — God was honoring Him! Being honored by God is promised to the one who dwells in the shelter of the Most High.

Summary

He will call upon Me, and I will answer him; I will be with him in trouble; I will rescue him, and honor him.

Depending upon their level of spiritual maturity, people usually call upon God for different reasons. Although there are times when God does not answer those who call upon Him, those who abide in the shadow of the Almighty are informed that they will call upon God and that He promises to answer them. God also promises to be with dwellers in times of trouble. He does not promise to remove the trouble but rather to be with them in the midst of their trouble. When dwellers find themselves in a position of having to trust God when their logic and reason can make no sense of the situation, God promises to rescue and honor them.

Psalm 91:16

A Long Satisfying Life

With a long life I will satisfy him,
And let him behold My salvation.

According to this last verse, dwellers will be satisfied or fulfilled with their length of life on earth. Matthew Henry remarks on this first phrase.

> They shall think it long enough; for God by his grace shall wean them from the world and make them willing to leave it. A man may die young, and yet die full of days, *satur dierum—satisfied with living.* A wicked worldly man is not satisfied, no, not with long life; he still cries, Give, give. But he that has his treasure and heart in another world has soon enough of this; he would not live always.[221]

Albert Barnes adds a comment.

> A time will come, even under this promised blessing of length of days, when a man will be "satisfied" with living; when he will have no strong desire to live longer; when, under the infirmities of advanced years, and under his lonely feelings from the fact

that his early friends have fallen, and under the influence of a bright hope of heaven, he will feel that he has had enough of life here, and that it is better to depart to another world.[222]

In the book of Genesis, Moses validates that the dweller lives a long, satisfied life by recording an epitaph concerning the life of Abraham.

> These are all the years of Abraham's life that he lived, one hundred and seventy-five years. Abraham breathed his last and died in a ripe old age, an old man and satisfied with life; and he was gathered to his people. (Genesis 25:7–8)

Scripture tells us that salvation is everlasting.[223] Remember, life does not end at the grave, although our final destiny has been determined by the time we enter death's door. Life goes on throughout eternity, which would certainly qualify as a "long life." Albert Barnes makes this comment concerning the last phrase of Psalm 91:16:

> In another life, after he shall be "satisfied" with this life. The promise extends beyond the grave: "Godliness is profitable unto all things, having promise of the life that now is, and of that which is to come." Thus, religion blesses man in this life, and blesses him forever. In possession of this, it is a great thing to him to live long; and then it is a great thing to die—to go to be forever with God.[224]

The book of Proverbs addresses the issue of wisdom and adds important insight.

> She is more precious than jewels; And nothing you desire compares with her. Long life is in her right hand; in her left hand are riches and honor. (Proverbs 3:15–16)

In the course of his life, a dweller is taught by the Lord and therefore gains wisdom and understanding. According to Proverbs, wisdom brings a long life and honor. Both wisdom and honor are promised to the one who dwells in the shelter of the Most High.

> **With a long life I will satisfy him,**
> ***And let him behold My salvation.***

What is the salvation that God will let the dweller behold? According to Isaiah, the LORD GOD is our salvation.

> "Behold, God is my salvation, I will trust and not be afraid; For the LORD GOD is my strength and song, and He has become my salvation." (Isaiah 12:2)

The New Testament tells us that in the city of Jerusalem, there was a righteous, devout man named Simeon who was in the temple on the day Mary and Joseph brought Jesus to be presented to the Lord. Simeon took the infant Jesus into his arms. The words he spoke have been recorded.

> "Now Lord, Thou dost let Thy bond-servant depart in peace, according to Thy word; For my eyes have seen Thy salvation." (Luke 2:29–30)

When Simeon saw Jesus, he announced that he had seen the salvation of the Lord. The book of Hebrews tells us that Jesus Christ is the author of our salvation.[225] The book of Acts offers this confirmation concerning Jesus:

> "And there is salvation in no one else; for there is no other name under heaven that has been given among men, by which we must be saved." (Acts 4:12)

Although the disciples were privileged to physically rub shoulders with Jesus during His time on earth, we have not had that opportunity. Yet Psalm 91:16 tells us that God will let the dweller behold His salvation. To *behold* means to "see, look at, inspect, perceive, and consider."[226] Since Jesus is the source of eternal salvation,[227] we need to look to Him. We need to look at, inspect, perceive, and consider His life. By so doing, we are able to behold the salvation of God. In the Gospel of John, Jesus gave a comforting promise.

> "In My Father's house are many dwelling places; if it were not so, I would have told you; for I go to prepare a place for you. And if I go and prepare a place for you, I will come again, and receive you to Myself; that where I am, there you may be also." (John 14:2–3)

> "I will not leave you as orphans; I will come to you." (John 14:18)

When we receive the Lord Jesus Christ as our personal Savior, we become believers and enter into the kingdom of heaven through His salvation. As believers, we have been predestined to be conformed into His image.[228] As we grow and mature in our faith, we become more like Him. One day Jesus Christ will return for His bride. Then when time is no more and we enter into the realm of eternity, we will behold Him face-to-face.

Summary

With a long life I will satisfy him,
And let him behold My salvation.

God has taught dwellers to trust Him over the years of their lives, and they have become overcomers. They have chosen to dwell in the shelter of the Most High and have discovered—at least in part—what it means to abide in the shadow of the Almighty. As a result, dwellers will be satisfied with their lives. They are not attached to this world and are aware they are just passing through. In the interim, they have had the privilege of beholding the salvation of God. In the life to come—whenever that may be—they look forward to seeing their God face-to-face.

Psalm 91

Summary

Psalm 91 has taken us on an interesting journey. The beginning of this psalm provides the reader with a condition and a promise. The condition involves the would-be dweller in a way of life that is far removed from the mundane. The goal of dwelling is to prepare a Christian to abide in the shadow of the Almighty.

The New Testament book of Romans refers to an interesting transformation in the life of a Christian.

> I urge you therefore, brethren, by the mercies of God, to present your bodies a living and holy sacrifice, acceptable to God, which is your spiritual service of worship. And do not be conformed to this world, but be transformed by the renewing of your mind, that you may prove what the will of God is, that which is good and acceptable and perfect. (Romans 12:1–2)

The Greek word *metamorphoo* is translated as "transformed" in Romans 12:2. We get the word *metamorphosis* from that word. A metamorphosis is to take place in the life of a Christian. Christians are transformed—or undergo a metamorphosis—when their minds are renewed. The process might be likened to the transformation of a caterpillar into a butterfly.

As Christian individuals make the choice to dwell in the shelter of the Most High, God initiates a training program unmatched by secular or religious institutions. God's curriculum is designed to adequately prepare each individual for His intended purpose. To ensure success God tests not only a person's knowledge but also the intent of the heart. As Christians begin appropriating the characteristics of God as their own, God continues to hone and refine them as they become more conformed into the likeness of the Lord Jesus Christ. As they abide in the shadow of the Almighty, they will become a malleable, useful instrument in the hands of the Lord.

The Purpose and Advantage of Dwelling

As we review the results of dwelling in the shelter of the Most High and abiding in the shadow of the Almighty, we are reminded that there are those who would not prefer to take the journey. Nevertheless, those who choose to undergo the journey will be able to stand firm on the promises of God, and they will find their faith growing as their knowledge and love for God increases. Carefully ponder each statement below, and ask God to reveal your heart as you contemplate the implications of Psalm 91.

As a Dweller ...

1. You will dwell in the shelter of the Most High and abide in the shadow of the Almighty.

2. You enter into a covenant relationship with the Lord and accept Him as your refuge and fortress. You will learn to put your trust in God, not in your own ability, knowledge, or resources.

3. You will be delivered from the snare of the trapper and from the deadly pestilence.

4. His truth and faithfulness will be your protection and will cover you.

5. You will not fear what the enemy brings your way. Nor will his arrows pierce you.

6. What you learn will protect you from any pestilence the enemy tries to put upon you.

7. Although others may have fallen at the hand of their enemies, you will still be standing when the smoke of battle clears.

8. You will witness spiritual enemies getting their just reward.

9. When the Lord becomes your refuge and the Most High your dwelling place, a major transition will take place in your life.

10. The enemy's evil words will not penetrate your soul. You will thwart the attacks of the enemy in your own life and will not be defeated in your spiritual battles.

11. You will have a special group of angels to watch over, guard, and keep you on track.

12. Your angels will support you. You are not tripped up along the way.

13. You will trample down your enemies regardless of their size, demeanor, or strength.

14. You will truly love God. He will deliver you and set you in a safe, inaccessible place out of your enemies' reach because you know His name.

15. When you call upon God, He will answer. You can be assured that He will be with you in troubling times.

16. You will be satisfied with your life and will behold the salvation of the Lord.

Making the choice to dwell in the shelter of the Most High and to abide in the shadow of the Almighty is not an act that should be done in fear and trepidation. In and of itself, it is an act of worship. It should also be an act of faith as we make our vows to God. The book of James provides a pertinent message.

> Submit therefore to God. Resist the devil and he will flee from you. Draw near to God and He will draw near to you. Cleanse your hands, you sinners; and purify your hearts, you double-minded. (James 4:7–8)

What James is saying dovetails into what the psalmist has recorded in Psalm 91. As we make the choice to dwell, we are agreeing to submit to God's will even though our emotions may not always be in accord with that decision. In other words, we are making the choice to submit to God. We know that we can trust Him regardless of wherever He would lead.

James sets the stage for something very significant.

> For we all stumble in many ways. If anyone does not stumble in what he says, he is a perfect man, able to bridle the whole body as well. (James 3:2)

When a man is walking or running, he can stumble. He can be tripped, or he can even fall. When we *stumble* in what we say, it means "to err, to make a mistake ... to sin in word or speech."[229] In other words, if what we say lines up with God's truth, we will not stumble. However, if we say something that is not true but act as though it is true, we have stumbled. An example of this is given in an account recorded by Luke, the beloved physician. Ananias and Sapphira had sold a piece of property and decided to retain a portion of the sales for themselves, yet they act as if they had given everything for the apostles to disperse among the needy. Peter addressed the issue in Acts 5.

> "Ananias, why has Satan filled your heart to lie to the Holy Spirit, and to keep back some of the price of the land? While it remained unsold, did it not remain your own? And after it was sold, was

it not under your control? Why is it that you have conceived this deed in your heart? You have not lied to men, but to God." (Acts 5:3–4)

Ananias and Sapphira stumbled in what they said. The words that came out of their mouths did not line up with what was in their hearts. James tells us that if we do not stumble in what we say, we are perfect people—that is, we are fully-grown, mature. Obviously, Ananias and Sapphira did not meet those criteria.

A Practical Application

After Christians make the Psalm 91:2 declaration to the Lord, there may be times when they find themselves in a troubling situation and are tempted to return to their old habits of dealing with trying issues. We find David in a disturbing situation in Psalm 143.

> For the enemy has persecuted my soul; He has crushed my life to the ground; He has made me dwell in dark places, like those who have long been dead. Therefore my spirit is overwhelmed within me; My heart is appalled within me. (Psalm 143:3–4)

Although not fruitful, it is common to think upon and ponder our negative situation. If demons are involved, they will add fuel to the fire by contributing their thoughts and feelings to the equation. Should we choose to accept demonically induced thoughts and feelings as a true indicator of reality, the demons gain the right to continue their destructive assault. Should the world or the flesh be allowed a voice, we have a recipe for a major disaster.

Dwellers are not super saints. They are human. Nonetheless, they do have tools at their disposal that will enable them to counteract the negative forces from the world, the flesh, and the kingdom of darkness that are coming against them. Psalm 143 reveals that David utilized some of those tools and put them to good use.

> Let me hear Thy lovingkindness in the morning; for I trust in Thee; Teach me the way in which I should walk; For to Thee I lift up my soul. Deliver me, O LORD, from my enemies; I take refuge in Thee. Teach me to do Thy will, For Thou art my God; Let Thy good Spirit lead me on level ground. For the sake of Thy name, O LORD, revive me. In Thy righteousness bring my soul out of trouble. (Psalm 143:8–11)

Instead of pondering his current situation, David purposefully forced his mind to change direction and remembered former days while meditating on the goodness of God. His soul longed for and sought after the LORD. He trusted in God instead of trusting in the nagging thoughts and feelings that had him in a pit of despair. He desired to be obedient to God and asked Him to bring his soul out of trouble.

As dwellers, we would do well to follow David's example by committing our soul to the One we have chosen to trust as our refuge and fortress. It may be that we are being tested in order to determine the intent of our heart. Will we truly rely upon God as our refuge and fortress in the face of adversity, or will we act as though He is nowhere to be found and revert to our own resources?

By the time we have made the Lord our dwelling place, we will be equipped to overcome any plot the enemy may throw our way. We have learned to walk in the ways of the Lord and to take our thoughts captive. We have likewise learned to tread upon some rather formidable spiritual foes that purpose to derail us. We can be assured that the Lord will hear and answer when we call upon Him. He will be with us in trouble and will rescue us.

When you need to seek refuge or when you find yourself in need of a divine rescue, you can make the choice to deliver your soul into the care of the divine Caretaker. When trouble strikes, you have come to a fork in the road. You can choose to take the path that leads to defeat, or you can take the path that leads to the defeat of the enemy.

When we apply the words we speak to the first two verses of Psalm 91, the seriousness of what we utter comes into sharp focus. We are telling the LORD—the One who condemns unrighteousness, pronounces judgment, and metes out punishment on the offenders—that He is our refuge and fortress. We tell Him He is our God. He is the One we trust!

Proverbs 17 adds to the equation.

> The refining pot is for silver and the furnace for gold, but the LORD tests hearts. (Proverbs 17:3)

When we say such things as Psalm 91:1–2 to the Lord, He takes it very seriously. He will use adversity to test our words to see what is in our heart, and He will thus determine if we truly rely upon Him as our refuge and fortress. If it is our heart's desire for the Lord to be our refuge and fortress, God will put us through the curriculum He knows we need to enable the dross to be removed. James informs us we should be elated when various trials come our way. The testing of our faith produces endurance, which, in turn, leads to maturity in the faith.[230]

Psalm 91 highlights the growth and maturity of the one who dwells in the shelter of the Most High, thus enabling him to abide in the shadow of the Almighty.

At this stage of your journey through Psalm 91, it should be apparent that you have an opportunity to enter into a covenant relationship with the Lord that goes far beyond entering into the kingdom of heaven through salvation. The Psalm 91 covenant presses the would-be dweller toward maturity. A *covenant* is defined as "a written agreement or promise usually under seal between two or more parties especially for the performance of some action."[231] The biblical record is full of evidence showing that

God always upholds His end of a covenant. Should you choose to enter into the Psalm 91 covenant with God, He will expect you to honor what you say. In this study we have looked at the promise a dweller makes to the Lord, at God's curriculum, and at what He promises the dweller. Before a covenant becomes binding, however, it must be ratified. It must be approved, sanctioned, or confirmed formally. With that in mind, carefully consider the following declaration:

My Personal Declaration

Father, in the name of the Lord Jesus Christ, I desire to be all that You have created me to be. I do not know the future details that my particular journey to become a dweller may entail, but I know that I can trust You as we travel together. I am aware that various circumstances may occur that may challenge my logic, my reason, or my understanding. I know that you will test me to know my heart and to strengthen my faith. I am also aware that at times my mind or emotions may object to the curriculum I will need to encounter. Regardless, in making my vow to You, You will expect me to honor it, and I will. I know the Holy Spirit will teach me what I need to know in order to put the enemy to flight in my own life and will lead me in the way I need to go. Psalm 91:1–2 say,

He who dwells in the shelter of the Most High Will abide in the shadow of the Almighty. I will say to the LORD, "My refuge and my fortress, My God, in whom I trust!" (Psalm 91:1–2)

I know You have begun a good work in my life, so I choose to make the following declaration: "In sincerity and humbleness of heart, I make the choice to dwell in the shelter of the Most High so that I can abide in the shadow of the Almighty. I choose the Lord as my refuge and my fortress. You are my God in whom I trust!"

Name _____

Date _____

Notes

Prayer

You may find the following prayer a helpful guide any time you need to seek refuge from the Lord or whenever you find yourself in a situation requiring a divine rescue.

> Father, you know all the negative thoughts that are bombarding my mind and the feelings that would overwhelm me. I reject these thoughts and feelings. I take authority over and bind the enemies that have brought them. If I have listened to any lies, thoughts, or feelings of the world, the flesh, or demons, I confess that as sin and ask You to forgive me. I take back all the ground I may have given to the enemy, and I give that ground back to the Lord Jesus Christ. I break any curses that may have been put on me. I command these oppressive demonic spirits to leave me and to go where the Lord Jesus Christ wants them to go.
>
> I choose to set my mind and dwell on those things that are true, honorable, right, pure, lovely, and of good repute.[232] Father, I ask You to hide my soul in the secret place of your tent. I choose to dwell in the shelter of the Most High so that I can abide in the shadow of the Almighty.
>
> All this I pray in the name, the power, and the authority of the Lord Jesus Christ.
>
> Amen.

Notes

Bibliography

Adeyemo, Tokunboh. *Africa Bible Commentary.* The Zondervan Corporation.

Andrew Jukes. *The Names of God Discovering God As He Desires To Be Known.* Grand Rapids: Kregel Publications, 1967.

Bubeck, Mark. *The Adversary.* Chicago: Moody Press, 1975.

Myers, Rick *e-Sword* Version 7.9.7. (http://www.e-sword.net/)

Adam Clark's Commentary on the Bible.

Albert Barnes's Notes on the Bible.

Brown-Driver Briggs's Hebrew Definitions.

John Gill's Exposition of the Entire Bible New Modern Edition.

Potter, Areon. *From Darkness to Light.* Bloomington, IN: WestBow Press.

Ryrie, Charles Caldwell. *The Ryrie Study Bible* NASB. Chicago: Moody Press, 1978.

Stone, Nathan. *Names of God.* Chicago: Moody Press, 1944.

Strong, James. *The New Strong's Expanded Dictionary of Bible Words.* Thomas Nelson Publishers.

Tenney, Merrill C. ed. *The Zondervan Pictorial Bible Dictionary.* Grand Rapids: Zondervan Publishing House, 1967.

Thayer, Joseph Henry. *Thayer's Greek-English Lexicon of the New Testament*. Grand Rapids: Baker Book House, 1977.

Vine. *Vine's Complete Expository Dictionary of Old and New Testament Words*. Thomas Nelson Publishers 1996.

Scripture Index

Endnotes

Psalm 91:1: Dwelling in the Shelter of the Most High (Part 1)

1   Corinthians 10:21.

2   Taken from *Vine's Complete Expository Dictionary of Old and New Testament Words* by W. E. Vine, Merrill F. Unger, William White, Jr. Copyright © 1984, 1996 by W. E. Vine, Merrill F. Unger, William White, Jr. Used by permission of Thomas Nelson (www.thomasnelson.com).

3   Taken from *Vine's Complete Expository Dictionary of Old and New Testament Words* by W.E. Vine, Merrill F. Unger, William White, Jr. Copyright © 1984, 1996 by W.E. Vine, Merrill F. Unger, William White, Jr. Used by permission of Thomas Nelson (www.thomasnelson.com).

4   Romans 8:9.

5   1 Thessalonians 5:23; Hebrews 4:12.

6   The story is found in 2 Samuel 11.

7   You can read the full report in 2 Samuel 12.

8   Jonah 2:10.

9   Numbers 13:17–14:10.

10 For a better understanding of the names of God, refer to chapter 8 titled "Names of God" in the author's first book, *From Darkness to Light*.

11 Genesis 14:19–20.

12 2 Corinthians 11:14.

13 Mark 5:1–13.

14 Mark 5:7.

15 Philippians 2:11.

16 Rick Myers, e-Sword, Brown-Driver-Briggs's Hebrew Definitions, Electronic Edition on Psalm 91:1, Strong's #5643. (https://www.e-sword.net/).

17 By Permission. From Merriam-Webster.com. Copyright © 2017 by Merriam-Webster, Inc. https://www.merriam-webster.com/dictionary/secret.

18 Taken from *Vine's Complete Expository Dictionary of Old and New Testament Words* by W. E. Vine, Merrill F. Unger, William White, Jr. Copyright © 1984, 1996 by W. E. Vine, Merrill F. Unger, William White, Jr. Used by permission of Thomas Nelson (www.thomasnelson.com).

19 Rick Myers, e-Sword, Albert Barnes's Notes on the Bible, Electronic Edition. (https://www.e-sword.net/).

20 By Permission. From Merriam-Webster.com. Copyright © 2017 by Merriam-Webster, Inc. https://www.merriam-webster.com/dictionary/secreted.

21 John 4:24.

22 1 Corinthians 6:17.

23 Psalm 5:4.

24 1 John 5:18.

Psalm 91:1: Abiding in the Shadow of the Almighty (Part 2)

25 Taken from *Vine's Complete Expository Dictionary of Old and New Testament Words* by W. E. Vine, Merrill F. Unger, William White, Jr. Copyright © 1984, 1996 by W. E. Vine, Merrill F. Unger, William White, Jr. Used by permission of Thomas Nelson (www.thomasnelson.com).

26 Genesis 19:8.

27 Taken from *The New Strong's Expanded Dictionary of Bible Words* by James Strong Copyright © 2001 by James Strong. Used by permission of Thomas Nelson (www.thomasnelson.com).

28 Exodus 20:5.

29 See the author's first book *From Darkness to Light* for a more in-depth study in dealing with the iniquities of the fathers.

30 Galatians 5:19–21.

31 1 Peter 1:18.

32 1 Corinthians 15:33.

33 To learn how to deal with an evil soul tie, refer to the author's first book, *From Darkness to Light*, chapter 9, part 1.

34 Mark Bubeck, *The Adversary* (Chicago: Moody Press, 1975), 47.

35 John 16:33.

36 Joseph Henry Thayer, *Thayer's Greek-English Lexicon of the New Testament* (Grand Rapids: Baker Book House, 1977), 291, Strong's # 2347. Public Domain.

37 Taken from *Vine's Complete Expository Dictionary of Old and New Testament Words* by W. E. Vine, Merrill F. Unger, William White, Jr. Copyright © 1984, 1996 by W. E. Vine, Merrill F. Unger, William White, Jr. Used by permission of Thomas Nelson (www.thomasnelson.com).

38 Rick Myers, e-Sword, Albert Barnes's Notes on the Bible, Electronic Edition on Colossians 2:8. (https://www.e-sword.net/).

39 Romans 12:2.

40 2 Corinthians 4:4.

41 1 John 3:10.

42 By Permission. From Merriam-Webster.com. Copyright © 2017 by Merriam-Webster, Inc. https://www.merriam-webster.com/dictionary/usurp.

43 Joseph Henry Thayer, *Thayer's Greek-English Lexicon of the New Testament* (Grand Rapids: Baker Book House, 1977), 569, 571. Public Domain.

44 Taken from *Vine's Complete Expository Dictionary of Old and New Testament Words* by W. E. Vine, Merrill F. Unger, William White, Jr. Copyright © 1984, 1996 by W. E. Vine, Merrill F. Unger, William White, Jr. Used by permission of Thomas Nelson (www.thomasnelson.com).

45 Nathan Stone, *Names of God* (Chicago: Moody Press, 1944) 40.

46 Nathan Stone, *Names of God* (Chicago: Moody Press, 1944), 38, 39.

47 Nathan Stone, *Names of God* (Chicago: Moody Press, 1944), 34.

Psalm 91:2: The Declaration

48 By Permission. From Merriam-Webster.com. Copyright © 2017 by Merriam-Webster, Inc. https://www.merriam-webster.com/dictionary/vow.

49 Also see Ecclesiastes 5:4 and Psalm 50:14.

50 Charles Caldwell Ryrie, *The Ryrie Study Bible* NASB (Chicago: Moody Press, 1978), on Genesis 2:4.

51 Taken from *The Zondervan Pictorial Bible Dictionary* by Merrill C. Tenney Copyright © 1963, 1964, 1967 by Merrill C. Tenney. Use by permission of Zondervan (www.zondervan.com)

52 Nathan Stone, *Names of God* (Chicago: Moody Press, 1944), 44.

53 Genesis 2:18–21.

54 Rick Myers, e-Sword, Matthew Henry's Commentary on the Whole Bible, Electronic Edition on Psalm 91:2. (https://www.e-sword.net/).

55 See Numbers 15:38–39 (NIV).

56 Read 2 Samuel 22:1–2, Psalm 18:2, and Psalm 144:1–2.

57 Charles Caldwell Ryrie, *The Ryrie Study Bible* NASB (Chicago: Moody Press, 1978), on Genesis 1:1.

58 Genesis 1:1–25.

59 Genesis 1:26.

60 Taken from *The Names of God: Discovering God As He Desires To Be Known.* Copyright © 1967 by Andrew Jukes. Published by Kregel Publications, Grand Rapids, MI. Used by permission of the publisher. All rights reserved.

61 Charles Caldwell Ryrie, *The Ryrie Study Bible* NASB (Chicago: Moody Press, 1978). See Ryrie's notes on Genesis 8:14.

62 By Permission. From Merriam-Webster.com. Copyright © 2017 by Merriam-Webster, Inc. https://www.merriam-webster.com/dictionary/ trust.

63 Taken from *The New Strong's Expanded Dictionary of Bible Words* by James Strong. Copyright © 2001 by James Strong. Used by permission of Thomas Nelson (www.thomasnelson.com).

64 Rick Myers, e-Sword, John Gill's Exposition of the Entire Bible, Electronic Edition on Psalm 143:3. (https://www.e-sword.net/).

65 Rick Myers, e-Sword, Albert Barnes's Notes on the Bible, Electronic Edition on Psalm 143:3. (https://www.e-sword.net/).

66 For a more thorough study of how demons work in the life of a Christian, read the author's first book titled *From Darkness to Light.*

67 By Permission. From Merriam-Webster.com. Copyright © 2017 by Merriam-Webster, Inc. https://www.merriam-webster.com/dictionary/ overwhelmed.

68 By Permission. From Merriam-Webster.com. Copyright © 2017 by Merriam-Webster, Inc. https://www.merriam-webster.com/dictionary/ meditate.

69 By Permission. From Merriam-Webster.com. Copyright © 2017 by Merriam-Webster, Inc. https://www.merriam-webster.com/dictionary/ muse.

70 John 17:15.

71 John 17:17.

72 Ephesians 6:11.

73 Ephesians 6:16.

74 2 Thessalonians 3:3.

75 1 John 2:13–14.

76 By Betty Spooner. Copyright 1982, *The Eagle.*

77 Matthew 12:34.

Psalm 91:3: It Is He Who Delivers You

78   Rick Myers, e-Sword, Brown-Driver-Briggs's Electronic Edition on Psalm 91:3, Strong's #H5337. (https://www.e-sword.net/).

79   Rick Myers, e-Sword, Treasury of David on Psalm 91:3. (https://www.e-sword.net/).

80   Job 1:1–2:7.

81   Matthew 17:14–20.

82   Luke 9:1.

83   Ephesians 6:10–18.

84   Deuteronomy 28:21.

Psalm 91:4: He Will Cover You

85   Rick Myers, e-Sword, Albert Barnes's Notes on the Bible, Electronic Edition on Exodus 19:4. (https://www.e-sword.net/).

86   Rick Myers, e-Sword, Strong's #H2620. (https://www.e-sword.net/).

87   By Permission. From Merriam-Webster.com. Copyright © 2017 by Merriam-Webster, Inc. https://www.merriam-webster.com/dictionary/believe.

88   Rick Myers, e-Sword, Albert Barnes's Notes on the Bible, Electronic Edition on Psalm 91:4. (https://www.e-sword.net/).

Psalm 91:5: You Will Not Be Afraid (Part 1)

89   By Permission. From Merriam-Webster.com. Copyright © 2017 by Merriam-Webster, Inc. https://www.merriam-webster.com/dictionary/fear.

90   Job 4:12–14.

91   Psalm 64:3–4.

92   1 Corinthians 10:20–21.

93   For more information on learning how to deal effectively with demonic oppression, read the author's book *From Darkness to Light*, which deals with demonic oppression and the Christian.

Psalm 91:6: You Will Not Be Afraid (Part 2)

94 By Permission. From Merriam-Webster.com. Copyright © 2017 by Merriam-Webster, Inc. https://www.merriam-webster.com/dictionary/stalk.

95 Rick Myers, e-Sword, Brown-Driver-Briggs's Electronic Edition on Psalm 91:6, Strong's #H652. (https://www.e-sword.net/).

96 Job 2:7.

97 Luke 13:11.

98 Psalm 78:49. KJV: evil angels. NASB: destroying angels.

99 By Permission. From Merriam-Webster.com. Copyright © 2017 by Merriam-Webster, Inc. https://www.merriam-webster.com/dictionary/stalk

100 See Psalm 143:3, 2 Corinthians 4:4, 2 Corinthians 11:3, and 1 John 2:11.

101 1 Corinthians 10:20–21.

102 Rick Myers, e-Sword, Strong's #H6986. (https://www.e-sword.net/).

103 Rick Myers, e-Sword, Brown-Driver-Briggs's Electronic Edition on Psalm 91:6, Strong's #H7703. (https://www.e-sword.net/).

104 Romans 6:23.

105 Genesis 3:16.

106 Genesis 3:17–19.

107 Genesis 2:25.

Psalm 91:7: A Thousand May Fall

108 1 Timothy 3:7.

109 Romans 8:37 (KJV).

Psalm 91:8: The Reward of the Wicked

110 Genesis 3:14.

111 Isaiah 14:14.

112 Joseph Henry Thayer, *Thayer's Greek-English Lexicon of the New Testament* (Grand Rapids: Baker Book House, 1977), 77, #746, 2. Public Domain.

113 The story is found in Mark 5:1–13.

114 Taken from *The New Strong's Expanded Dictionary of Bible Words* by James Strong. Copyright © 2001 by James Strong. Used by permission of Thomas Nelson (www.thomasnelson.com).

115 Joseph Henry Thayer, *Thayer's Greek-English Lexicon of the New Testament* (Grand Rapids: Baker Book House, 1977), 225, Strong's #1849. Public Domain.

116 Taken from *Vine's Complete Expository Dictionary of Old and New Testament Words* by W. E. Vine, Merrill F. Unger, William White, Jr. Copyright © 1984, 1996 by W. E. Vine, Merrill F. Unger, William White, Jr. Used by permission of Thomas Nelson (www.thomasnelson.com).

117 Charles Caldwell Ryrie, *The Ryrie Study Bible* (Chicago: Moody Press, 1978), on Daniel 10:12.

118 Joseph Henry Thayer, *Thayer's Greek-English Lexicon of the New Testament* (Grand Rapids: Baker Book House, 1977), 530, #4189. Public Domain.

Psalm 91:9 The Commitment

119 Romans 7:25.

120 1 Corinthians 6:17.

121 Taken from *The Zondervan Pictorial Bible Dictionary* by Merrill C. Tenney. Copyright © 1963, 1964, 1967 by Merrill C. Tenney. Use by permission of Zondervan (www.zondervan.com).

122 Romans 7:22.

123 1 Chronicles 21:1–8.

124 Matthew 4:1–11.

125 Ephesians 6:16.

126 2 Corinthians 10:5.

127 Ephesians 6:18.

128 Luke 9:1.

129 James 4:7; Mark 5:1–13.

130 Leviticus 19:2.

131 Psalm 14:6, Psalm 142:5, and Jeremiah 16:19.

132 Psalm 91:14.

133 Read Genesis 14:18–20.

134 Proverbs 3:33.

Psalm 91:10: No Evil Will Befall You

135 The thoughts that bombard your mind may be worded in the first-person singular. "Hasn't God said in Psalm 91 that no evil will befall me? It seems to me this situation I am in is very evil. Well, the promise in Psalm 91:10 may be good for someone else, but it is obviously not meant for me. The truth of the matter is that I am not so sure God does care about me or my situation."

136 Rick Myers, e-Sword, Brown-Driver-Briggs's Hebrew Definitions, Electronic Edition on Psalm 91:10, Strong's #H7451. (https://www.e-sword.net/).

137 Taken from *The New Strong's Expanded Dictionary of Bible Words* by James Strong. Copyright © 2001 by James Strong. Used by permission of Thomas Nelson (www.thomasnelson.com).

138 Taken from *The Zondervan Pictorial Bible Dictionary* by Merrill C. Tenney. Copyright © 1963, 1964, 1967 by Merrill C. Tenney. Use by permission of Zondervan (www.zondervan.com).

139 Genesis 37:2.

140 Thirty years old plus seven years of plenty plus two years of famine equals thirty-nine years. See Genesis 41:46, 53; 45:6.

141 See Genesis 47:28.

142 Rick Myers, e-Sword, Brown-Driver-Briggs's Hebrew Definitions, Electronic Edition on Psalm 91:10, Strong's #H579. (https://www.e-sword.net/).

143 1 Samuel 19:15.

144 Matthew 14:8–11.

145 Matthew 27:22–58.

146 Matthew 26:53.

147 Rick Myers, e-Sword, Strong's word #7931. (https://www.e-sword.net/).

148 Rick Myers, e-Sword, John Gill's Exposition of the Entire Bible, Electronic Edition on Proverbs 1:33. (https://www.e-sword.net/).

149 Matthew 12:34.

150 Galatians 5:24.

151 1 Corinthians 9:27; Luke 22:42.

152 1 Corinthians 6:17.

153 It was defeated in verse 7 of Psalm 91.

154 2 Corinthians 12:7.

155 Matthew 4:1–11.

156 Deuteronomy 7:12–15.

157 Deuteronomy 28:58–62.

158 Taken from *The New Strong's Expanded Dictionary of Bible Words* by James Strong. Copyright © 2001 by James Strong. Used by permission of Thomas Nelson (www.thomasnelson.com).

159 James 4:7.

Psalm 91:11: The Angels' Commission

160 Excerpt from David Wilkerson's letter of 11/15/2004 (www.worldchallenge.org).

161 Charles Caldwell Ryrie, *The Ryrie Study Bible* (Chicago: Moody Press, 1978), on 1 Kings 18:21.

162 Daniel 10:12–13, 21.

163 James 4:7.

Psalm 91:12: They Will Bear You Up

164 1 Kings 18:22, 40.

165 By Permission. From Merriam-Webster.com. Copyright © 2017 by Merriam-Webster, Inc. https://www.merriam-webster.com/dictionary/strike.

166 Revelation 20:3.

167 Rick Myers, e-Sword, Albert Barnes's Notes on the Bible, Electronic Edition on Matthew 4:7. (https://www.e-sword.net/).

Psalm 91:13: You Will Tread Upon

168 Joshua 10:12–14.

169 Hosea 11:10.

170 Psalm 17:12.

171 Proverbs 28:1; 30:30.

172 Isaiah 31:4.

173 Areon Potter, *From Darkness to Light* (Bloomington, IN: WestBow Press), xv.

174 Rick Myers, e-Sword, John Gill's Exposition of the Entire Bible, Electronic Edition on Luke 10:19. (https://www.e-sword.net/).

175 Rick Myers, e-Sword, Adam Clarke's Commentary on the Bible, Electronic Edition on Luke 10:19. (https://www.e-sword.net/).

176 By Permission. From Merriam-Webster.com. Copyright © 2017 by Merriam-Webster, Inc. https://www.merriam-webster.com/dictionary/trample down.

177 For further study, see the author's first book, *From Darkness to Light*, chapter 7, part 3.

Psalm 91:14: Because He Has Loved Me

178 Taken from Africa Bible Commentary by Tokunboh Adeyemo. Copyright © 2006 by Tokunboh Adeyemo. Use by permission of Zondervan (www.zondervan.com).

179 Rick Myers, e-Sword, Strong's word #H2836. (https://www.e-sword.net/).

180 Genesis 34:8; Deuteronomy 21:11.

181 Psalm 78:11.

182 Psalm 103:7.

183 Hebrews 6:10.

184 Psalm 9:10.

185 Taken from *The New Strong's Expanded Dictionary of Bible Words* by James Strong. Copyright © 2001 by James Strong. Used by permission of Thomas Nelson (www.thomasnelson.com).

186 Joseph Henry Thayer, *Thayer's Greek-English Lexicon of the New Testament* (Grand Rapids: Baker Book House, 1977), 653, #5368. Public Domain.

187 Taken from *Vine's Complete Expository Dictionary of Old and New Testament Words* by W. E. Vine, Merrill F. Unger, William White, Jr. Copyright © 1984, 1996 by W. E. Vine, Merrill F. Unger, William White, Jr. Used by permission of Thomas Nelson (www.thomasnelson.com).

188 Joseph Henry Thayer, *Thayer's Greek-English Lexicon of the New Testament* (Grand Rapids: Baker Book House, 1977), 3, 4, #25. Public Domain.

189 Rick Myers, e-Sword, Albert Barnes's Notes on the Bible, Electronic Edition on Psalm 91:14. (https://www.e-sword.net/).

190 Author's paraphrase.

191 Rick Myers, e-Sword, Brown-Driver-Briggs's Hebrew Definitions, Electronic Edition on Psalm 91:14, Strong's #6403. (https://www.e-sword.net/).

192 Rick Myers, e-Sword, Brown-Driver-Briggs's Hebrew Definitions, Electronic Edition on Psalm 92:8, Strong's #4791. (https://www.e-sword.net/).

193 2 Kings 21:1–3.

194 Rick Myers, e-Sword, Brown-Driver-Briggs' Hebrew Definitions, Electronic Edition on 2 Kings 21:3, Strong's #1116 and refers to elevation as in a high place. (https://www.e-sword.net/).

195 Rick Myers, e-Sword Strong's #7311. See also Genesis 7:17. (https://www.e-sword.net/).

196 Rick Myers, e-Sword, Brown-Driver-Briggs's Hebrew Definitions, Electronic Edition on Psalm 91:14, Strong's #7682. (https://www.e-sword.net/).

197 See Psalm 57:1; 121:7; and 143:8, 11.

198 For a more thorough explanation of the names of God, see author's first book, *From Darkness to Light*, chapter 8, part 1.

199 Psalm 9:9–10.

200 1 Samuel 17:45.

201 Romans 8:29.

Psalm 91:15: He Will Call upon Me

202 Joseph Henry Thayer, *Thayer's Greek-English Lexicon of the New Testament* (Grand Rapids: Baker Book House, 1977), 610, #4982. Public Domain.

203 1 Corinthians 3:1–3.

204 Exodus 3:10–11.

205 Matthew 16:13–22.

206 By Permission. From Merriam-Webster.com. Copyright © 2017 by Merriam-Webster, Inc. https://www.merriam-webster.com/dictionary/perplex.

207 This is also true of the spiritual Christian.

208 Job 5:17.

209 Jeremiah 23:5–6.

210 Proverbs 17:17.

211 James 2:23.

212 Psalm 37:4.

213 Deuteronomy 11:16–17.

214 1 Kings 16:29–33.

215 By Permission. From Merriam-Webster.com. Copyright © 2017 by Merriam-Webster, Inc. https://www.merriam-webster.com/dictionary/initiate.

216 Psalm 66:18; Isaiah 59:2.

217 Rick Myers, e-Sword, Strong's #6869. (https://www.e-sword.net/).

218 Rick Myers, e-Sword, Brown-Driver-Briggs's Hebrew Definitions, Electronic Edition on Numbers 31:3, Strong's #2502. (https://www.e-sword.net/).

219 Romans 8:37 (KJV).

220 1 Samuel 2:30.

Psalm 91:16: A Long, Satisfying Life

221 Rick Myers, e-Sword, Matthew Henry's Commentary on the Whole Bible, Electronic Edition on Psalm 91:16. (https://www.e-sword.net/).

222 Rick Myers, e-Sword, Albert Barnes's Notes on the Bible, Electronic Edition on Psalm 91:16. (https://www.e-sword.net/).

223 Isaiah 45:17.

224 Rick Myers, e-Sword, Albert Barnes's Notes on the Bible, Electronic Edition on Psalm 91:16. (https://www.e-sword.net/).

225 Hebrews 2:10.

226 Rick Myers, e-Sword, Brown-Driver-Briggs's Hebrew Definitions, Electronic Edition on Psalm 91:16, Strong's #H7200. (https://www.e-sword.net/).

227 Hebrews 5:9.

228 Romans 8:29.

Psalm 91: Summary

229 Joseph Henry Thayer, *Thayer's Greek-English Lexicon of the New Testament* (Grand Rapids: Baker Book House, 1977), 556, #4417. Public Domain.

230 James 1:2–4.

231 By Permission. From Merriam-Webster.com. Copyright © 2017 by Merriam-Webster, Inc. https://www.merriam-webster.com/dictionary/covenant.

Psalm 91: Prayer

232 Philippians 4:8.

Printed in the United States
By Bookmasters